pretty in patchwork

holidays

30+ SEASONAL PATCHWORK PROJECTS TO PIECE, STITCH, AND LOVE

john q. adams

LARK CRAFTS
Asheville

Editor: Amanda Carestio

Assistant Editor: Thom O'Hearn

Copyeditor: Nancy Wood

Art Directors: Megan Kirby & Amy Sly

Art Production: Celia Naranjo

Illustrators: Aimee Ray (how-to) &

Orrin Lundgren (stitches and templates)

Photographers: Susan Wasinger &

Steve Mann

Cover Designer: Celia Naranjo

LARK CRAFTS

An Imprint of Sterling Publishing
387 Park Avenue South
New York, NY 10016

If you have questions or comments about
this book, please visit: larkcrafts.com

Library of Congress Cataloging-in-Publication Data

Pretty in patchwork : 30+ seasonal patchwork projects / John Q. Adams.
    p. cm.
  Includes bibliographical references and index.
  ISBN 978-1-4547-0279-5 (alk. paper)
  1. Christmas decorations. 2. Patchwork. I. Adams, John Q., 1974- II. Title: Seasonal
patchwork projects. III. Title: 30+ seasonal patchwork projects.
  TT900.C4.P757 2012
  745.594'12--dc23
                                      2011047741

10 9 8 7 6 5 4 3 2 1

First Edition

Published by Lark Crafts
An Imprint of Sterling Publishing Co., Inc.
387 Park Avenue South, New York, NY 10016

Text © 2012, John Q. Adams
Photography © 2012, Lark Crafts, an Imprint of Sterling Publishing Co., Inc., unless
otherwise specified
Illustrations © 2012, Lark Crafts, an Imprint of Sterling Publishing Co., Inc., unless
otherwise specified

Distributed in Canada by Sterling Publishing,
c/o Canadian Manda Group, 165 Dufferin Street
Toronto, Ontario, Canada M6K 3H6

Distributed in the United Kingdom by GMC Distribution Services,
Castle Place, 166 High Street, Lewes, East Sussex, England BN7 1XU

Distributed in Australia by Capricorn Link (Australia) Pty Ltd.,
P.O. Box 704, Windsor, NSW 2756 Australia

Manufactured in China

ISBN 13: 978-1-4547-0279-5

For information about custom editions, special sales, and premium and corporate
purchases, please contact Sterling Special Sales Department at 800-805-5489 or
specialsales@sterlingpub.com.

Requests for information about desk and examination copies available to college
and university professors must be submitted to academic@larkbooks.com. Our
complete policy can be found at www.larkcrafts.com.

table of contents

greetings!

Yes, I am one of those people. I start thinking about the holidays before our swimsuits are packed away for the season. The Christmas music starts before we even purchase the Thanksgiving turkey. And yes, I go shopping at the crack of dawn on Black Friday, and I don't rest until every last one of those gifts is meticulously wrapped.

But what can I say? I love the holidays. It's a time to celebrate family, to reconnect, to share, and to make gifts…and memories, of course. For me, there is a clear connection between the holidays and the creation of handmade items. Each presents a special way to celebrate those you love and share a bit of yourself with them.

That's why the process of putting together this book has been such a labor of love—thinking through the many ways to incorporate a passion for sewing and crafting into holiday celebrations, and collaborating with so many talented sewists and designers to bring those ideas to life. The projects all sit at the intersection of family, holiday, and handmade. Who wouldn't want to hang out for a bit at that intersection? Especially when patchwork is thrown into the mix!

In these pages you'll find 28 patchwork projects to make for yourself, your home, or someone special, all created to celebrate the season: from home decor to gift ideas to table dressings for your holiday feasts. Oh, and quilts, of course. Quilts are key to setting the stage for a homemade holiday. Think pieced trees and penguins, modern spins on traditional blocks, fun patchwork letters and sayings, reusable gift wrap, adorable polar bears, hedgehogs, and gingerbread men… And among all that goodness, I've sprinkled in some seriously cute mini ornament projects for quick crafting.

I've also included a few fall items, which can work from October straight through the December holidays and beyond. Best of all, many of these projects can be altered slightly through color palette and fabric choice, to work year-round or for other holidays. And we've given plenty of ideas for simple variations along the way.

Whatever projects within these pages you may choose to create, or however this book inspires you, I hope you are able to patch together a little bit of homemade into your holiday celebrations.

John Q. Adams, Quilt Dad

the basics

From small to large, simple-to-sew to intricate and complex, traditional to modern, "quick fix" to long-term projects, and wonky and improvisational to precise, there's a project in this book for every taste and skill level. Because I wanted this book to be inclusive of all quilters and sewists from beginner to more experienced, I felt it was important to include a robust basics chapter. Besides, even an old dog can learn a new trick or two!

The following pages should come in handy if you find yourself needing a quick lesson—or refresher—in piecing, quilting, binding, and some of the other techniques used in the projects.

the materials

Let's face it: if you're anything like me, shopping for the materials for a new project is probably one of, if not the most, enjoyable parts of the crafty process. In fact, I wouldn't be surprised if you already have a stash of materials ready to go. I know I do! But just in case, let's take a quick tour through the basic list of materials needed for most of the projects in this book.

fabric

Ahh, fabric. It gets me every time! The process of selecting fabrics—mixing and matching different prints and colors—is what drew me to sewing in the first place. It enabled me to express myself in a way I hadn't experienced before. I'm always surprised to see that the step of choosing fabrics can be paralyzing to new sewists for fear of "messing it up." I try to advise them to follow their instinct and, as simplistic as it sounds, to just choose what they love. The rest will all come together.

Sometimes I select my fabrics first, and then search for (or come up with) the perfect pattern to show them off. Other times, I fall in love with a pattern and then seek out the fabrics that I think will let that pattern sing. Neither way is "right" or better than the other. Let inspiration strike you whenever and wherever it can.

It's often easiest for a new quilter to find a particular fabric line or collection that they like, and use fabrics from that collection to complete their project. There is absolutely nothing wrong with that! After all, there is a skilled and talented designer pulling that collection together, paying attention to the colors and the assortment of prints and the scale of the designs. Fabric lines are designed to work well and look great together.

As your skill level and confidence grows, it's natural to break beyond the barriers of a single fabric collection and start mixing and matching prints and colors from a lot of different lines. This is the part of the process where many quilters truly find their creative voice, and it's the part of the process I like best. I think you'll see that some of the projects in this book are all made from a single line (or collection) of fabric, while others showcase the designer's method and skill of combining fabrics together.

When selecting fabrics for a new quilt project, I like to follow my own "Rule of 5":

1 **A large-scale print:** This is often the print I am drawn to first, and it usually serves as the jumping off point from which I will select supporting prints and colors.

2 **Small-scale prints:** I pick these to complement (but not necessarily match) the large-scale print.

3 **Dots and stripes:** These are great pieces to build out the dimers on of the finished project.

4 **Solids:** I typically like to find two or three solids to pull the prints together.

5 **The X-factor:** This is that little bit of unexpected whimsy that helps you add your signature style to the project. It could be a novelty print or something completely unexpected. Think outside the box!

Make your fabric selections according to the Rule of 5, and you're well on your way! Consider these rules when building a fabric stash too, to help ensure a healthy assortment of fabric for any quilting project.

threads & embroidery floss

I have to admit: I am NOT a thread snob. In fact (and please don't revoke my quilter's card), thread is probably the supply I pay least attention to. Give me a nice big spool of all-cotton thread in white or off-white, and I am good to go. Many sewists enjoy having a large assortment of types and colors of thread on hand to match to their fabric choices for any given project. This can also come in handy when machine quilting your project.

Remember, though, that a contrasting thread can be just as effective as a matching thread. In fact, I often prefer the look of a more visible, contrasting top-stitch on a project.

Embroidery floss is perfect for, well, embroidery, and the price is so affordable that it's worth it to "stash up" and build a fun, colorful stock of thread to shop from when working on an embroidery project. And though I'm not a hand quilter myself, embroidery floss and perle cotton are both great options for hand quilting.

batting

When I first began sewing (and didn't know any better), I always purchased extra high-loft polyester batting. I figured that it was all about the loft. And you know what? I never had any issue with it.

As I've learned more about quilting and quilting materials, I've come around to using 100% cotton batting. I simply like the thought of using all-natural materials whenever possible. I will say, though, that it took me a while to get used to it. Cotton batting produced a much thinner quilt than I was expecting, and at first I thought my quilts were too thin. Now, I'm one of the converted, and nothing washes and dries up better than a quilt made with cotton batting.

fabric cuts

For me—and, I assume, for many new quilters—terms like "fat quarter" and "fat eighth" can be a bit confusing. Here's a quick vocabulary lesson:

Assuming fabric on the bolt is 44 inches (111.8 cm) wide, a standard quarter-yard cut of fabric would measure 9 x 44 inches (22.9 x 111.8 cm). However, many quilters don't like these standard cuts. Sometimes you lose too much of a repeating pattern to be useful, or maybe the long narrow cut is too restrictive in the ways you can use the fabric. So quilters, being the ingenious bunch that we are, thought of a different way to cut up fabric. Hello, fat quarter!

Fat quarters measure 18 x 22 inches (45.7 x 55.9 cm)—a ¼ yard (.2 m) of fabric, but cut in a much more user-friendly way than a quarter yard cut off the bolt, which would measure 9 x 44 inches (22.9 x 111.8 cm).

Fat eighths follow the same cutting philosophy but take it one step further, cutting each fat quarter in half to create 9 x 22-inch (22.9 x 55.9 cm) fabric pieces.

the tools

Sewing and quilting tools (or "notions") are great and all kinds of fun, but I've really stuck to the K.I.S.S. method of collecting tools: "keep it simple, (insert derogatory name-calling word here)." Really, you can create nearly anything with the most basic tools—provided, of course, that you select the right ones. Don't get me wrong: I'm not against all of the fun rulers and gadgets that are designed to make your life easier, so feel free to get as geared up as you want!

Take a look at right for my list of "must-haves."

And of course, there are a few "fun-to-haves" that can make your quilting experience that much more enjoyable.

- Graph paper and pencils: I use these when designing or figuring out new project and patterns.
- Specialty rulers, like angle and shape rulers
- Various sewing feet for your machine: If you're going to invest in any, I'd suggest a walking foot first, followed by a darning foot for free-motion quilting.
- Embroidery kit (needles, hoops, water soluble pen, floss, and transfer tools)
- Hand-sewing needles
- Fusible web and interfacing
- My laptop for playing my favorite tunes, multitasking, and on-the-fly tweeting and blogging while sewing

basic patchwork tool kit

- Sewing machine
- Rotary cutting system (cutter, mat, and an assortment of transparent quilting rulers)
- Scissors (sewing and craft)
- Straight pins and quilter's pins (Though, I admit, I rarely ever use pins.)
- Ironing board and iron (My tip: buy the biggest ironing board that fits into your space and budget—it'll be worth it.)
- Seam ripper (Though I try my darndest to never have to use it.)
- Thread
- Tools for your preferred method of basting (I prefer spray basting adhesive, though curved basting pins are the classic choice.)

the techniques

Now that you've got your tools, are you excited to get started? Let's get ready to sew! Whether this is your first attempt at patchwork or you're already a seasoned pro, the basics are really just that: basic. Once you master these few easy techniques, the rest is all about practice and self-confidence.

templates

All of the templates that you need to make the projects in this book are included, and you'll find them at the back of the book. Simply enlarge the templates according to the percentages provided and then use them as instructed in the project pattern. If you have a scanner and printer, then you won't even need a trip to the copy shop!

cutting

The majority of these projects utilize a rotary cutter, a self-healing mat, and a clear quilting ruler or two. I sewed for years with only two rulers: a 6 x 24-inch (15.2 x 61 cm) rectangular grid ruler, and a small 1 x 6-inch (2.5 x 15.2 cm) ruler. These are still my two "go-to" rulers, and I am convinced you can tackle any quilting project with these simple tools.

I also have a single rotary cutter and self-healing mat. Again, while I know that collecting a variety of tools can be enjoyable, I think you can achieve everything you want with a few simple but smart selections. And if you have small children in the home like I do, I'd strongly recommend a rotary cutter with a locking safety mechanism.

The other cutting tools I really enjoy are clear square rulers. I use these rulers for two purposes: to square up quilt blocks and to fussy-cut designs for some of my quilt blocks and other projects (**A**).

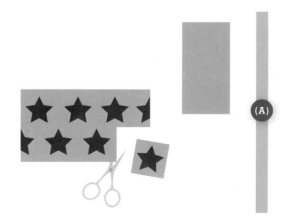

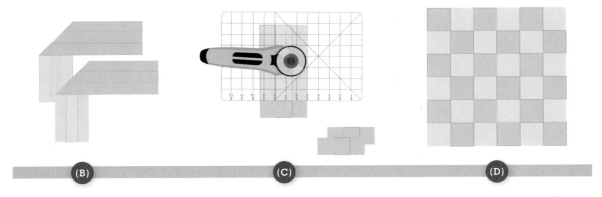

(B)   (C)   (D)

strips

Strip piecing is a tried and true way to efficiently use your time and materials. When a pattern calls for a lot of small piecing, consider this quick tip for piecing strips that will have even a beginner looking like a patchwork pro.

1 Stitch a group of strips together. Press **(B)**.

2 Cut those pieced strips into strips **(C)**.

3 Now rotate the orientation of the pieces, stitch those very same strips together again, and press **(D)**. You can also use this trick to create pieced segments that are used multiple times.

Chain piecing is another of my favorite techniques when sewing a lot of pieces together in a single sitting. Simply feed your pieces through the sewing machine one after another, leaving a little space between them. When you're done, you'll have a "chain" of sewn-together pieces that simply need to be snipped apart before continuing on to your next step.

the log cabin

I've got lots of love for log cabins! The log cabin quilt block is one of the oldest and most traditional of blocks, yet its high degree of flexibility makes it easy to update and modernize. Let's review the basics: A log cabin block consists simply of a block center surrounded by square or rectangular "logs."

1 Start by cutting a center square **(E)**.

2 Sew a log, either square or rectangular, to one side of the block center **(F)**.

3 Moving in one direction, either clockwise or counterclockwise, continue adding logs until your block is the desired size **(G)**.

Whether straight or wonky, symmetrical or off-kilter, modern or traditional, scrappy or planned, square or otherwise, learn to love the log cabin block! I promise it will become a staple of your patchwork repertoire.

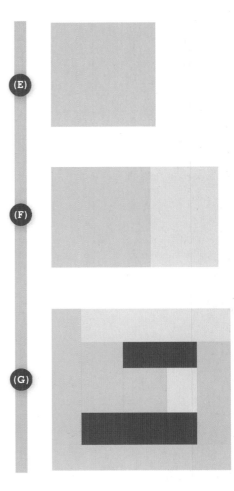

(E)   (F)   (G)

english paper piecing

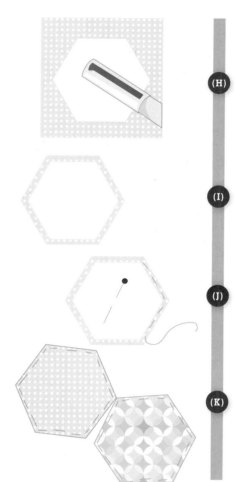

I have to admit, English paper piecing isn't one of my favorite techniques, but I know some people love it. It's a great on-the-go project, and it produces hexagonal patchwork that's a nice contrast to the more traditional squares and rectangles.

When it comes to English paper piecing, perfection and precision are fundamental. With the aid of paper templates and a few tips, you may learn to enjoy this most impressive technique.

1 First, carefully cut a number of paper templates. You can save some time and find precut shapes online or make them yourself with basic word processing or presentation software.

2 Place the templates on the wrong side of the fabric and cut around each, leaving a ¼-inch (6 mm) allowance on all sides **(H)**.

3 Fold the seam allowance over the edges of the template **(I)**, and then press them in place using a steam iron or just your fingers; using just your fingers helps to make the project more portable!

4 Baste the edges in place **(J)**, working only through the fabric corners and edges or directly through the paper.

5 Press well for a nice, crisp edge.

6 Once you've basted all of your hexagons, attach them, right sides together, at the edges **(K)** using a ladder stitch (page 13). Remove the paper templates.

appliqué

I have another confession: I avoid handwork like the plague. I do enjoy a small embroidery project every now and then, but hand sewing and me … well, we just don't get along that well. The term "needle-turn appliqué" strikes terror into my heart. So when it comes time to incorporate some appliqué into my projects, fusible interfacing is my best friend. With this handy tool, adhering appliquéd shapes to your project is as simple as ironing them on the background.

Don't forget to machine or hand stitch around your shape to secure your appliqué, because I've found that the fusing often weakens during a machine wash. Here are a few ways to ensure that your appliqué remains securely attached to your project:

A simple straight stitch **(L)** can do the job easily while leaving the edges raw, or turn the edges under—nice and neat!—using the freezer paper method **(M)**. Explore additional stitches, like zigzag or decorative stitches, to add another element to your design.

embroidery

Despite my aversion to handwork, I have really grown to love hand embroidery as a way to embellish my quilting and sewing projects. All you really need is your fabric, a hoop, a needle, and a couple of colors of embroidery floss. Once you have a design—either your own or someone else's—you're good to go. Just follow these easy steps to get started on your first or next embroidery project.

transferring patterns & prepping fabric

Once you have chosen an image to embroider, there are a variety of ways to transfer that image to fabric. The method that has worked the best for me is also the simplest: simply lay the fabric over top of a printed copy of the image and trace with a water-soluble marker. If the image can't easily be seen and you don't have a lightbox on hand, try the DIY method: tape the paper up on a sunny window and use the natural light to your advantage! Other tools to help with your transfer include fabric transfer paper, pens, and pencils.

Once your image is transferred to fabric, you're ready to start stitching! While you're "hooping up" your fabric (plastic or wood—I've used both), let's review some common stitches.

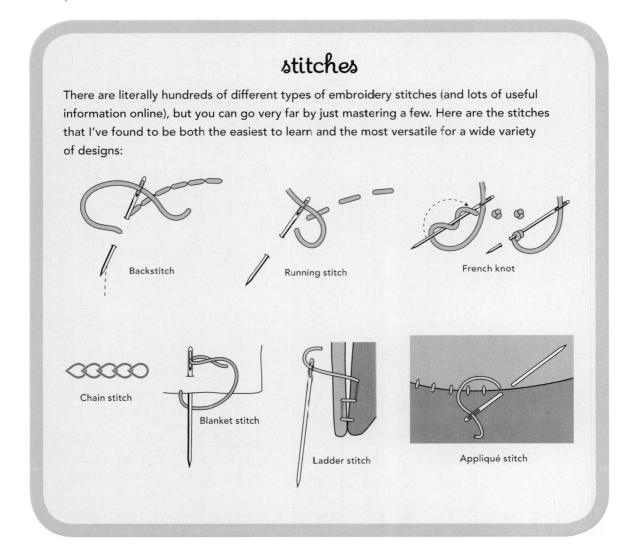

stitches

There are literally hundreds of different types of embroidery stitches (and lots of useful information online), but you can go very far by just mastering a few. Here are the stitches that I've found to be both the easiest to learn and the most versatile for a wide variety of designs:

Backstitch

Running stitch

French knot

Chain stitch

Blanket stitch

Ladder stitch

Appliqué stitch

quilting

The most basic definition of a quilt is "a blanket made of two layers of fabric with a soft material between them, stitched in patterns or tufted through all layers in order to prevent the filling from shifting." And while we place a great deal of emphasis on constructing the quilt top—surely the focal point of most quilts—it's the final step of quilting that often brings the piece to life. Alas, it's also the step that many sewists find the most challenging. So let's review the basics…and hopefully remove some of the anxiety about quilting.

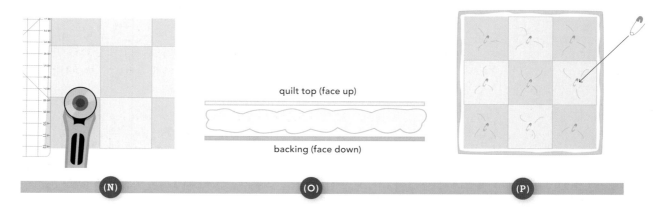

quilt top (face up)

backing (face down)

(N)　　　　(O)　　　　(P)

the quilt sandwich

Ready to turn your piece of patchwork into an actual quilt? The first step is mastering the art of the quilt sandwich. The ingredients? A quilt top that is smooth, freshly pressed, and squared up to the right measurements **(N)**, a layer of batting, your quilt back (also freshly pressed), and your basting tools of choice.

On a flat surface, lay the quilt backing wrong side up. Some people like to secure the backing down by taping the corners to a hard, flat surface (like a wood floor) with painter's tape. Next, layer the batting on top, smoothing it out from the center. Finally, lay your quilt top atop the batting with its right side up **(O)**. Secure (or "baste") all three layers together with basting pins or spray, beginning in the center and working outward to the edges, smoothing as you go **(P)**.

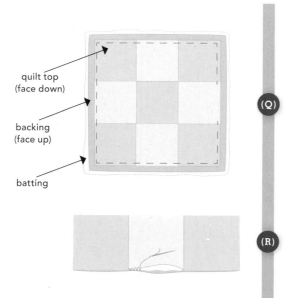

quilt top
(face down)

backing
(face up)

batting

(Q)

(R)

Before I was comfortable making the quilt sandwich, I used a method of finishing my quilts called the **quick-turn method**, or "birthing" the quilt. This is a great way for beginning quilters to finish their quilts, because it eliminates the often-intimidating step of binding the quilt. Here's how I did it:

1 Lay the batting down first, then the quilt backing (right side up), followed by the quilt top (right side down). Smooth each layer as you go **(Q)**.

2 Pin around the outside edge, smoothing as you go.

3 Using a ½-inch (1.3 cm) seam allowance, stitch around the outside edge of the quilt, leaving an 6-inch (15.2 cm) opening for turning.

4 With a rotary cutter or scissors, carefully trim the layers along the edges and across the corners to decrease the bulk.

5 Turn the quilt right side out. Handstitch the opening closed **(R)**.

6 Quilt as desired.

stitching

With your quilt sandwich assembled and secured, it's time for the step that gives a quilt its name: the quilting! There are many different ways to quilt a quilt: machine stitching, tying, hand quilting, or having the quilt finished by a long-arm quilter. When finishing the quilt yourself on your home machine, there are a few basic quilting techniques that will be good to know.

Stitch in the Ditch: If you want your quilting to be virtually invisible, allowing the fabrics to take center-stage, you may want to "stitch in the ditch" by actually stitching into the seams of the patchworked fabric **(S)**.

Straight Line Stitching: Stitch vertical and/or horizontal straight lines, preferably with a walking foot **(T)**. You can use a quilting bar attachment for perfectly spaced quilting lines, or use your quilting ruler and water soluble pen to draw guidelines for your quilting. Alternatively, let your lines be a little less than straight—you might like the wonky and modern look it gives you.

Free-Motion Stitching: Free motion quilting is the perfect solution for quilters who are unable to draw a straight line or color inside the lines! If you're equipped with a darning foot and a decent sense of rhythm, drop your feed dogs and consider giving free motion quilting a try. Guide the quilt sandwich through the sewing machine to create an all-over stippling pattern **(U)**. The trick is to keep a nice steady rhythm, both in the speed of your stitching (no lead feet!) and the speed at which you're guiding your fabric through the machine. Don't like the look of stippling? Try quilting other free-form shapes, pictures, or words into your design. Think of it as drawing with your sewing machine.

You can also add all kinds of handmade appeal to your projects with hand quilting and tying.

binding

I'm finally ready to admit this: the mere thought of binding a quilt was almost enough to scare me away from quilting altogether. After using the quick-turn method on my first few quilts though, I knew it was time to take the leap.

When it comes to binding, quilters typically fall into one of two camps: those for whom binding is their most favorite part of the quilt-making process, and those for whom it's their least favorite part. I guess I'd fall into the latter category, but I've learned the best ways to make binding a quilt work for me and my style. And besides, getting to the point when you're binding your quilt means you're nearly done.

The first step in binding a quilt is to create the binding strips, which is literally the fabric that will enclose your quilt. I always prefer making my own binding, mostly because it allows me to choose the colors and prints that I think will best complement my quilt design. After all, your binding ultimately will serve as the "frame" for your finished quilt!

make your own binding

1 To figure out how long your binding will need to be, use the dimensions of your quilt and add together the lengths of the four edges you are binding. Add to that number approximately 4 to 6 inches (10.2 to 15.2 cm) to give yourself some breathing room.

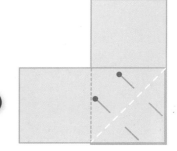

2 Refer to the pattern or project instructions for the recommended width of the binding strip, though I always cut my binding strips at 2½ inches (6.4 cm) wide. Cut strips from fabric or stitch several strips together to make a binding strip long enough for your project. Many quilters will recommend that you cut your binding strips on the bias, though I never do. Stitch the short ends of your strips together at a 45° angle **(V)**, right sides together, and press the seams open.

For patchworked binding, the ends are generally joined flush, end to end with right sides together **(W)**.

3 With wrong sides together, fold your binding strip in half, lengthwise. Press. Now you're ready to stitch on your binding.

double fold (or french) binding

1 Pin your newly-made binding strip (already folded and pressed in half lengthwise, wrong sides together) to the right side of the quilt top, lining up the raw edges.

2 Starting about 5 inches (12.7 cm) from the end of the binding strip **(X)**, stitch in place using the recommended seam allowance— typically ¼ inch (.6 cm)—stopping ¼ inch (.6 cm) from the first corner. Backstitch a few times to secure the thread. Clip the thread and remove the quilt from the sewing machine.

3 To miter the corner, fold the binding strip up at 45° toward the top of the quilt. Fold the strip back down and align it with the next side of the quilt. Begin stitching again **(Y)**, ¼ inch (.6 cm) in from the folded edge.

4 Continue stitching the binding along the quilt's edge, mitering each corner as you get to it.

5 Stop stitching about 6 inches (15.2 cm) from your starting point. Backstitch. Clip the threads and remove the quilt from the machine. Overlap the ends of the binding strips and trim them down until they overlap by ½ inch (1.3 cm). Stitch them together with right sides together. Cut the excess and press the seam open.

6 Stitch down this last section of the binding.

7 Fold the binding to the back of the quilt. Hold it in place (you can always pin it, if you'd like) and slipstitch the binding to the backside of the quilt, mitering the corners as you get to them.

Alternatively, you may want to machine stitch your binding on to the quilt. Again at the risk of having my quilter's card revoked, I'll tell you that I much prefer to machine stitch my binding on to my quilt. Aside from helping me with my aforementioned aversion to hand stitching, I actually quite prefer the look of the top stitching along my binding, much as I like the look of it in clothing.

The main difference from the above steps when machine binding a quilt is that I actually start by sewing the binding to the back side of the quilt, rather than the front. The reason I do this is so that when it is time to complete the final step of topstitching the binding on, I am working on the front of the quilt and can be much more conscious of the look and appearance of my straight line stitching.

Well, that's about it! Now it's time to move on to the fun stuff. Crank up the Bing Crosby, stir up a steaming mug of hot chocolate (extra marshmallows in mine, please), deck the halls, and get ready to sew. Just flip the page and see what my friends and I have pulled together for you. I hope you'll be inspired to infuse your holiday celebrations with some homemade patchwork fun!

read between the lines pillow

Comprised of simple strips and squares, this pillow is ingenious in its design; customize it easily with personalized messages, children's names, or for other holidays throughout the year.

handmade by **KELLY LAUTENBACH**

fabric & such

Assorted fabric scraps, including some solid white scraps (see Fabric Note)

1 yard (.9 m) of tan fabric (for sides and back)

1 piece of fabric (for backing the quilted strips), 18 x 22 inches (45.7 x 55.9 cm)

1 piece of batting, 18 x 22 inches (45.7 x 55.9 cm)

6 decorative buttons

Pillow form, 16 x 26 inches (40.6 x 66 cm)

tools

Basic Patchwork Kit (page 9)

finished size

29 x 15½ inches (73.6 x 39.4 cm)

seam allowance

¼ inch (6 mm) unless otherwise indicated

fabric note

Pick out a variety of patterned fabrics to use for the 23 pieced "lines" of your pillow. While you do not have to use 23 different fabrics, a good variety will yield a more colorful and fun pillow.

get started

1 Cut out the following pieces from the fabrics:

- From fabric scraps: 23 strips, each measuring 1½ x 20 inches (3.8 x 50.8 cm).

- From white fabric scraps: 1 strip measuring 1½ x 44 inches (3.8 x 111.8 cm) or cut and piece together scraps as needed.

2 Lay out the strips in a pleasing order. You might want to take a quick picture of this order to help you remember it. A few of the pieces (the strips between letters in a word) will be trimmed down later to a slimmer width. You will make and assemble the pillow in three blocks, with each HO as a block.

3 Make the first H:

- From the white strip(s), cut two segments that each measure 5½ inches (14 cm) long, and one segment that measures 1½ inches square (3.8 cm).

- Fold the first strip of the patterned fabric in half and cut it into two pieces of equal length. Stitch them to both short ends of one white 5½-inch (14 cm) segment to make the first leg of your H (**A**).

- Repeat with your second planned colored strip, stitching each half to the 1½-inch (3.8 cm) white segment, to make the center of the H.

- Fold, cut, and stitch your third colored strip to the remaining white segment.

- Do not worry that the three pieces are not the same length. Stitch the strips together so the sides of the H match up. (You will trim off the excess from the top and bottom later.)

4 Make the first O:

- From the white strip(s), cut two segments that each measure 5½ inches (14 cm) long and two segments that measure 2 inches (5.1 cm) long.

- Set the fourth colored strip aside for now (it will later become the space between the H and O), and cut the fifth colored strip in half as before to make two pieces of equal length.

Stitch them to both short ends of a long white segment at 45° angles to form the edges of the O **(B)**.

- For the center of the O, cut a 2½-inch (6.4 cm) segment off the end of the fifth colored strip, then cut what remains of that strip in half. Piece this strip together as shown **(C)**.

- Stitch the right side of the O in the same way as the left side, but with the 45° angles going in the opposite directions.

- Stitch the strips together so the sides of the O match up.

5 Take the colored strip set aside in step 4, and trim off ½ inch (1.3 cm) to make it 1 inch (2.5 cm) wide. Position it between the H and the O strips and stitch in place. Stitch the eighth strip to the right of the O to complete the first HO block.

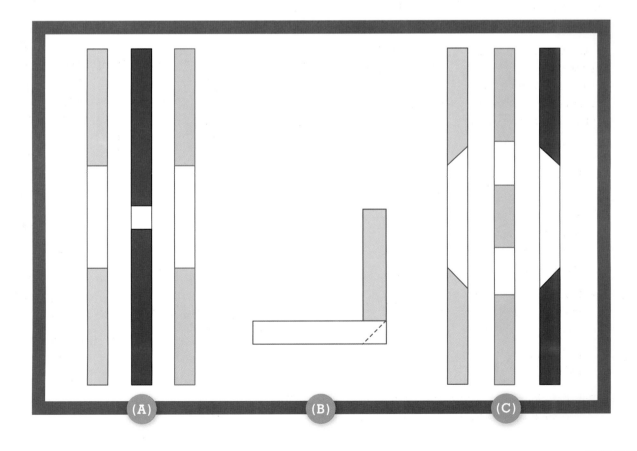

(A)   (B)   (C)

6 Repeat steps 3 through 5 to make two more HO blocks, using the colored strips in order according to your plan. The third HO block will not have a strip to the right of the O.

7 Attach the three blocks together to form one unit that reads HO HO HO. Take care to match up the tops of the letters and do not worry about the varying lengths of the strips. The finished width of this pieced strip should be approximately 19½ inches (49.5 cm).

8 Now you can trim off the ends! Measure 5½ inches (14 cm) up from the top of the letters and measure the same amount down from the bottom of the letters; use a rotary cutter, mat, and clear ruler to make straight cuts and trim away excess fabric.

9 Make a quilt sandwich with the pillow top, batting, and backing fabric, and quilt as desired (page 14–15). The sample shown uses the stitch in the ditch approach along the sides of each letter strip and around each letter.

10 Cut a piece of the tan fabric to the same dimensions as the pillow front. With right sides facing, stitch the two pieces together along the top and bottom edges only. This creates the central sleeve for the pillow.

11 Make the side flanges:

- From the tan fabric, cut two pieces that each measure 10½ x 31½ inches (26.7 x 80 cm).

- Form two tubes by stitching the short sides of each rectangle together with right sides facing. Turn the tubes right side out and press the seams.

- Lay each tube flat with the seam centered in the back of the tube, rather than at the top or bottom edge. Press.

- Make a double-fold hem on one side of both tubes.

- Use a disappearing fabric marker to measure and mark a buttonhole location on the front

of each flange, 2½ inches (6.4 cm) in from the hemmed edge and at the following points from the top edge: 3½ inches (8.9 cm), 7½ inches (18.4 cm), and 12 inches (30.5 cm).

12 Finish the pillow:

- Pin the flanges to both ends of the pillow. Make sure that the buttonholes are on the front of the pillow and the seam of the flange is on the back. Use the creases from when you pressed the tubes as a guide for pinning.

- Stitch both flanges in place. Turn the pillow right side out and press firmly.

- Hand sew the buttons to the flange, centering them behind the buttonholes.

- Insert the pillow form and button the sides closed.

spell it out

For a specific holiday or for a specific person, part of the fun of this design is that you can personalize it in so many ways. See page 122 for a construction chart for the rest of the letters of the alphabet.

modern maples throw quilt

Inspired by a traditional quilt block—the maple leaf—this throw quilt is made modern with the use of white space and fabric choice, including natural linen and a generous dose of fabric scraps.

handmade by **AMANDA WOODWARD-JENNINGS**

fabric & such

18 assorted fat quarters (45.7 x 55.9 cm) in autumn tones

3 yards (2.8 m) of background fabric

4½ yards (4.1 m) of fabric for backing

½ yard (.5 m) of fabric for binding

Double-size batting

tools

Basic Patchwork Kit (page 9)

finished size

59 x 70 inches (149.9 x 177.8 cm)

seam allowance

¼ inch (6 mm) unless otherwise indicated

get started

1 Cut out the following pieces from your fabric (A).

From each of the fat quarters:

- 3 squares for A-2, each measuring 4½ inches (11.4 cm).

- 2 squares that will become B-B squares, each measuring 5 inches (12.7 cm).

- 1 strip for the stem (D), measuring 2 x 7 inches (5.1 x 17.8 cm).

From the background fabric:

- 18 squares for A-1, each measuring 4½ inches (11.4 cm).

- 72 squares that will become B-B squares, each measuring 5 inches (12.7 cm).

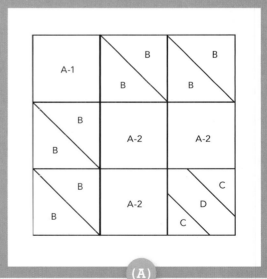

(A)

- 18 squares that will become C-D-C squares, measuring 4½ inches (11.4 cm); cut these squares in half diagonally (from corner to corner).

- 12 squares for the plain background blocks, each measuring 12½ inches (31.8 cm).

From the binding fabric, cut seven strips, each measuring 2¼ inches (5.7 cm) x the width of the fabric.

2 For each maple leaf block you will need to make four half-square triangles (the B-B blocks), each measuring 4 inches square (10.2 cm):

- With right sides facing, pin two 5-inch squares (12.7 cm) together, one background and one print.

- Use a pencil to mark a line from one corner of the square to the opposite diagonal corner.

- Stitch a seam ¼ inches (6 mm) from the pencil line, on both sides.

- Cut along the marked line. You now have two half-square triangles. Press seams to the print side.

- Repeat the process with another pair of 5-inch squares (12.7 cm).

3 For each maple leaf block, you will need to make one C-D-C block for the stem:

- With right sides facing, pin and stitch together one of the D strips to the long edge of one C triangle (B). Press the seam open.

- Pin, stitch, and press a second C triangle to the other side of the D strip in the same way.

- Trim down your block to 4½ inches square (11.4 cm). Your stems will be "liberated," meaning each one will be slightly different depending on how you square up each C-D-C block. Some can be more wonky than others, depending on personal preference.

4 Repeat steps 2 and 3 to make a total of 72 half-square triangles and 18 C-D-C blocks.

5 Following the diagram (C), lay out one complete maple leaf block:

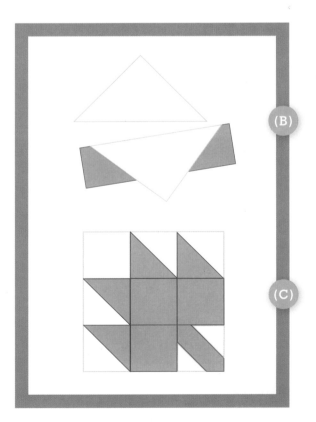

(B)

(C)

- Stitch together the rows from left to right, pressing the seams open.

- Lay row one on top of row two and pin liberally, matching the seams. Stitch together and press seams open.

- Attach row three in the same way.

- Repeat these steps to make all 18 blocks.

6 To assemble the quilt top:

- Following the photo, lay out the blocks on a design wall, floor, or bed. It helps to be able to see them in place, in case you want to change some blocks around.

- Start with the first row and stitch four maple leaves and one solid background block together. When sewing the maple leaf blocks together, line up the seams as best as you can and pin thoroughly. Press seams open.

- Stitch each row together, one at a time. Sometimes after the rows are completed, you might decide that you want to switch them around in the layout.

- Once your quilt is how you like it, start assembling the long rows into a quilt top, one row at a time. Press seams open.

7 Cut the backing fabric in half. Pin and stitch the long edges together. Press seams open.

8 Make a quilt sandwich with the quilt top, batting, and backing, baste, and quilt as desired (pages 14–15).

9 Stitch the binding strips together end-to-end to make one long strip and bind the quilt (pages 15–17).

drawstring gift bags

For many creative folks, a gift's packaging is often as important as the gift itself. Grab your favorite fabrics and present your gift in a thoughtful (and reusable) handmade bag, practically another present in itself!

handmade by JOHN Q. ADAMS

fabric & such *(to make one)*

1 fat quarter (45.7 x 55.9 cm) of red, green, or tan quilter's linen

3 fat quarters (45.7 x 55.9 cm) of lining fabric

White, red print, or assorted fabric scraps

Extra-wide double-fold bias tape, in coordinating colors

tools

Basic Patchwork Kit (page 9)

Large safety pin

finished size

9¾ x 11 inches (24.8 x 27.9 cm)

seam allowance

¼ inch (6 mm) unless otherwise indicated

get started

the swiss cross bag

1 Cut out the following pieces from the fabrics.

From red linen fabric:

- 4 squares, each measuring 2½ inches (6.4 cm).

- 2 rectangles, each measuring 2½ x 6½ inches (6.4 x 16.5 cm).

- 1 rectangle measuring 2½ x 10½ inches (6.4 x 26.7 cm).

- 1 rectangle measuring 4½ x 10½ inches (11.4 x 26.7 cm).

- 1 rectangle measuring 10½ x 12½ inches (26.7 x 31.8 cm).

From white fabric scraps:

- 2 squares, each measuring 2½ inches (6.4 cm).

- 1 rectangle measuring 2½ x 6½ inches (6.4 x 16.5 cm).

From lining fabric:

- 2 rectangles, each measuring 10½ x 12½ inches (26.7 x 31.8 cm).

2 To form the Swiss cross:

- Join together the red and white 2½-inch (6.4 cm) squares in rows, with the white square in the middle as shown (**A**).

- Stitch the white rectangle between the two rows. Press.

3 To piece the front of the bag:

- Join the 2½ x 6½-inch (6.4 x 16.5 cm) red rectangles to the left and right sides of the Swiss cross.

- Stitch the remaining 10½-inch-long (26.7 cm) rectangles above and below the cross as shown, and press.

4 Follow the Finishing Instructions to complete the bag (page 29).

the patchwork stripe bag

1 Cut out the following pieces from the fabrics.

From tan linen fabric:

- 2 rectangles, each measuring 5½ x 10½ inches (14 x 25.4 cm).

- 2 rectangles, each measuring 3½ x 10½ inches (8.9 x 25.4 cm).

From assorted fabric scraps: 20 squares, each measuring 2½ inches (6.4 cm).

From lining fabric: 2 rectangles, each measuring 10½ x 12½ inches (25.4 x 31.8 cm).

2 To piece the bag:

- Stitch together five assorted fabric squares in a row to make a 2½ x 10½–inch (6.4 x 25.4 cm) strip.

- Repeat with the remaining 15 squares to create three more strips. You will have two strips each for the front and back of the bag.

- Pair up and join two strips together along the 10½-inch (26.7 cm) sides. Repeat with the remaining two strips. You will have two pieced patchwork strips. Press all strips.

- Lay out the front and back panels as shown (**B**), with the wider tan rectangle at the top, the pieced patchwork strips in the middle, and the narrow tan rectangle at the bottom. Stitch the rows together and press.

3 Follow the Finishing Instructions to complete the bag (page 29).

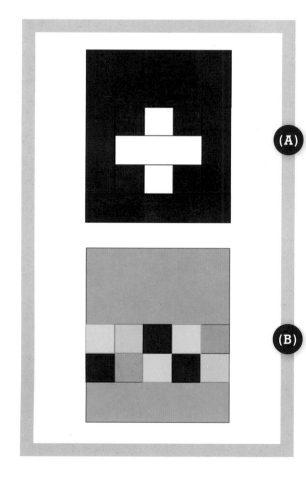

(A)

(B)

the wide stripe bag

1 Cut out the following pieces from the fabrics.

From green linen fabric:

- 2 rectangles, each measuring 5½ x 10½ inches (14 x 26.7 cm).

- 2 rectangles, each measuring 2½ x 10½ inches (6.4 x 26.7 cm).

From red print fabric: 2 rectangles, each measuring 5½ x 10½ inches (14 x 26.7 cm).

From lining fabric: 2 rectangles, each measuring 10½ x 12½ inches (26.7 x 31.8 cm).

2 For both front and back panels, lay out the fabrics using the project photograph as a guide (page 30), with the wide green rectangle at the top, the red print in the middle, and the narrow green at the bottom. Stitch the rows together and press.

3 Follow the Finishing Instructions to complete the bag (below).

finishing instructions for all versions

1 Make the lining:

- Pin the lining pieces with right sides together.

- Stitch around three sides, leaving the top 10½-inch (26.7 cm) edge open. Backstitch to lock the beginning and end of the stitches.

- Clip the corners without cutting the seam. Do not turn right side out. Set aside.

2 Join the exterior panels:

- Pin the two exterior panels with right sides together.

- On the right and left side of one panel, mark a line 1½ inches (3.8 cm) from the top and mark another 1 inch (2.5 cm) below the first mark.

- Stitch from the top of one side down to the first mark, backstitch, and cut the thread **(C)**. Start a new seam at the second mark and stitch around all three edges, stopping the next mark on the other side. Backstitch and cut your thread. Start a new seam at the fourth mark, backstitch, and stitch to the top edge.

- Clip the corners without cutting the seam.

- Press the seams open for the top half of each side of the bag exterior. Turn right side out and use a turning tool to push out the corners.

- Topstitch around each hole, securing the hole and catching the seam allowance on each side **(D)**.

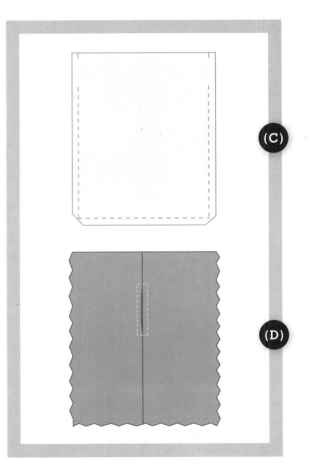

- Turn the bag right side out through the opening and push the lining into the exterior. Press the top of the bag, turning under and pressing the open part of the seam.

- Topstitch around the top edge of the bag to close the opening.

4 Create your drawstring casing:

- With a ruler and disappearing fabric marker, draw a straight line across the top of your bag directly underneath the holes on the sides of the bag. Draw this continuous line across both exterior panels so that they encircle the bag.

- Beginning on one of the side seams, topstitch along this marked line to create your drawstring channel. Be careful not to sew through all layers of the bag, but rather just the exterior and lining.

5 Create and insert the drawstrings:

- With the bias tape folded, use a matching thread to edge stitch the tape closed along its entire length.

- Cut the bias tape into two pieces, each measuring approximately 36 inches (91.4 cm) long.

- Attach a large safety pin onto the end of one piece of bias tape. Push the safety pin into the casing through one of the side openings and thread it around the entire bag until the safety pin reaches the same hole. Push through the opening and draw the bias tape evenly through the bag.

- Repeat this step using the remaining piece of bias tape, starting at the opening on the opposite side.

- Pull on the ends of the tape from both sides to gather the bag closed. Finish the tape ends with stitching or with knots.

3 Construct the bag:

- Slip the bag exterior inside the lining with right sides facing. Straighten out the exterior panels and push the corners into the corners of the lining, nestling them together for a nice, cozy fit. Pin the top edges together.

- Stitch around the top edge of the bags to join, leaving a 4-inch (10.2 cm) opening for turning, and backstitching to lock the beginning and end of the stitches.

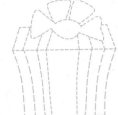

holiday surprise reverse appliqué pillow

This project combines three of my favorite things: pretty patchwork, a reverse appliqué technique, and a soft, comfy pillow that would look great with any holiday decor.

handmade by ANGELA MITCHELL

fabric & such

Assorted pieces of green fabric, at least 2½ inches square (6.4 cm)

1 yard (.9 m) of tan fabric (for background and backing)

½ yard (.5 m) of green solid fabric (for binding and trim)

½ yard (.5 m) of muslin (for inner pillow lining)

1 piece of batting, 19 inches square (48.3 cm)

Pillow form, 18 inches square (45.7 cm)

tools

Basic Patchwork Kit (page 9)

Template (page 121)

finished size

19 inches square (48.3 cm)

seam allowance

¼ inch (6 mm) unless otherwise indicated

get started

1 Cut the following pieces from the fabrics.

From the assorted green fabrics:

- 49 squares, each measuring 2½ inches square (6.4 cm).

From the background fabric:

- 1 square measuring 19 inches square (48.3 cm).

- 2 rectangles, each measuring 15 x 19 inches (38.1 x 48.3 cm).

From the green solid fabric:

- 4 strips measuring 2½ inches (6.4 cm) x the width of the fabric.

From the muslin:

- 1 square measuring 19 inches (48.3 cm).

2 Enlarge and cut out the tree template. Set aside.

3 To make the patchwork section:

- Lay out the assorted squares in seven rows of seven blocks.

- Stitch the first seven blocks together to make a row. Repeat for all seven rows.

- Press the seams in row one to the left, row two to the right, row three to the left, and so forth.

- Stitch the seven rows together to make a patchwork block that measures 14½ inches square (36.8 cm). Press seams open to reduce bulk.

4 Center the patchwork square on the batting (the patchwork square is smaller than the batting) and baste the pieces together. Machine quilt with straight lines ¼ inch (6 mm) from each horizontal and vertical seam.

5 To reverse-appliqué the pillow top:

- Make a quilt sandwich with the 19-inch (48.3 cm) background square on top (right side facing up), quilted patchwork square (right side facing up) in the middle, and muslin square on the bottom. Pin the layers together with one pin in each corner and one pin in the center.

- Flip the entire pillow top over, so the muslin side (pillow lining) faces up. Center and trace the template onto the pillow lining.

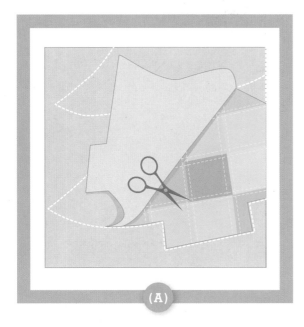

(A)

8 To complete the pillow:

- Lay the appliquéd pillow top with the right side facing down. Pin the prepared envelope backing pieces on top; the unfinished edges should align with the outer edges of the pillow top, and the green bound edges will overlap each other. Stitch together with a long basting stitch ⅛ inch (3 mm) from the outer edge.

- Bind the seam allowance around the pillow, mitering the corners (pages 15–17).

- Insert the pillow form through the envelope backing.

- Stitch the pillow top layers together by sewing along the tree outline three times. Do not try to sew exactly over your previous stitches.

- Flip the pillow top over again, with the muslin side down. Use a small pair of sharp scissors to cut out the tan fabric inside the tree outline (A). This will reveal your patchwork squares.

6 To prepare the envelope-style pillow backing:

- Cut one of the green solid strips into two 19-inch (48.3 cm) lengths. Press into double-fold binding.

- Bind one 19-inch (48.3 cm) raw edge on each piece of the 15 x 19-inch (38.1 x 48.3 cm) background fabric pieces.

7 Stitch the remaining solid green strips together end-to-end to make one long binding strip. Press into double-fold binding.

from the heart

Use different reverse appliqué shapes to celebrate other holidays throughout the year.

Itty Bitty Patchwork Ornaments

Enjoy working on a smaller scale? Then raid your scrap bucket and create a few of these mosaic-inspired holiday ornaments.

handmade by **CHRISTINA LANE**

fabric & such *(to make the set)*

Assorted print fabric scraps
¼ yard (.2 m) of linen
¼ yard (.2 m) of print fabric
Batting scraps
Paper-backed fusible web scraps
¼ yard (.2 m) of rickrack
Embroidery floss

tools

Templates (page 123)
Spray starch
Fray retardant
Pinking shears or pinking blade on a rotary cutter
Fabric glue

get started

1 The central appliqué of all the ornaments are cut from a grid of pieced squares. From fabric scraps, cut squares, each measuring 1 inch (2.5 cm) as follows:

- Dreidel: 54 squares from blue prints.
- Star: 56 squares from yellow prints.
- Tree: 54 squares from green prints.
- Snowman: 50 squares from white prints.

2 For each ornament, also cut one rectangle from the linen, the print fabric, and the batting, each measuring 6½ x 5½ inches (16.5 x 14 cm). Press and set aside.

3 Stitch the 1-inch (2.5 cm) squares together for each ornament as indicated by the template diagram. First stitch the squares into rows, then stitch the rows together. Press all seams open. Once fully assembled, lightly starch each piece and press with a hot iron.

4 To attach the fusible web:

- Lay a piece of fusible web over each ornament template and trace the shapes onto the paper

sides. Cut out each shape, leaving ¼ inch (6 mm) of fusible web beyond the outlines.

- Press each shape to the wrong side of the correct patchwork piece, following the manufacturer's instructions.

- With a pair of sharp scissors, cut around the traced ornament lines. To ensure minimal fraying on the patchwork, run a small bead of fray retardant around each piece.

5 To assemble each ornament, layer the linen and print pieces cut in step 2, wrong sides facing, with the cut batting pieces between, and press. Press the patchwork shapes, right side up, onto the linen side.

6 Using a sewing machine, stitch ⅛ inch (3 mm) around the outside of each shape and through all three layers. Clip the thread long enough to pull to the back of each piece and tie off. Using pinking shears or blade, cut out around each shape ¼ inch (6 mm) from the outline stitching.

7 To make the hanging loops, cut four pieces of rickrack, each measuring 8 inches (20.3 cm) long. Attach a loop of rickrack to the top of each ornament using glue and secure with a French knot using an embroidery needle and floss (page 13).

8 Using three strands of embroidery floss, stitch around the inner and outer edge of the patchwork piece ⅛ inch (3 mm) from the edge with a running stitch (page 13).

modern wreath baby quilt

A sweet gift idea for the newborns (or moms-to-be) in your life, don't think of this quilt as a gift for the holidays; instead, think of it as a gift for a lifetime.

handmade by JESSICA KOVACH

fabric & such

16 pieces of assorted green print fabrics, 5 inches square (12.7 cm)

16 pieces of assorted red print fabrics, 5 inches square (12.7 cm)

1¾ yards (1.6 m) of linen (for background and binding)

¼ yard (.23 m) of red fabric (for inner border)

⅜ yard (.34 m) of green fabric (for outer border)

1¼ yard (1.1 m) of backing fabric

1 piece of batting, 44 inches square (111.8 cm)

tools

Basic Patchwork Kit (page 9)

Templates (page 122)

finished size

41 inches square (104.1 cm)

seam allowance

¼ inch (6 mm) unless otherwise indicated

get started

1 Enlarge and cut out the templates, then cut out the following pieces from the fabrics.

From the linen:

- 4 binding strips, each measuring 2½ inches (6.4 cm) wide x the width of the fabric.
- 16 template A pieces.
- 16 template B pieces.
- 4 template D pieces.

From the assorted print fabrics:

- 16 template C pieces from the green print.
- 16 template C pieces from the red print.

From the red border fabric:

- 2 strips, each measuring 1¾ x 33½ inches (4.4 x 85.1 cm)
- 2 strips, each measuring 1¾ x 36 inches (4.4 x 91.4 cm)

From the green border fabric:

- 2 strips, each measuring 3 x 36 inches (7.6 x 91.4 cm)
- 2 strips, each measuring 3 x 41 inches (7.6 x 104.1 cm)

2 For each of the four blocks, collect the following fabric pieces:

- 4 linen A pieces.
- 4 linen B pieces.
- 8 total C pieces (four red and four green).
- 1 linen D piece.

3 Arrange the wreath shapes (template C pieces), alternating green and red fabrics. Surround the wreath with the A, B, and D pieces to form a complete block design.

4 To stitch one block:

- Select a wreath shape and its corresponding outer shape (which will be A or B). At the common edges, find the center by folding each piece in half and finger-pressing a crease at the center point. Reopen each piece.
- Pin the pieces together with right sides facing, matching up the crease marks. Pin the ends, allowing the A or B piece to overhang by ¼ inch (6 mm) for seam allowance.
- Pin the edges between the ends and the center, easing the fabric as you pin (A). You might need make ⅛-inch (3 mm) snips along the curved edge of A or B to help ease the curve.

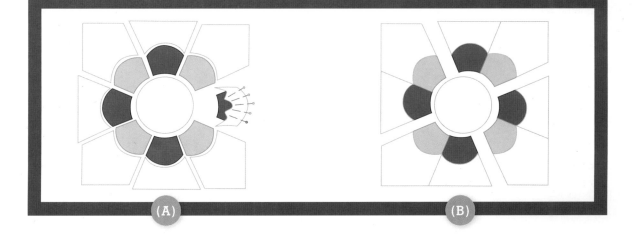

(A)   (B)

- Carefully stitch the two pieces together and press the seams away from the center of the wreath.

- Repeat for all eight wedges of the wreath.

5 Ignoring the center circle for now, stitch the wedge shapes together to construct the wreath shape. It helps to stitch two corner pairs together first, then connect the pairs (B). Press seams open.

6 Prepare the center circle (template D) by folding it in half and finger-pressing a crease on the fold. Open it back up and match the crease mark while folding it in half again, at another angle; finger-press two more creases. Repeat the process until you have marked off eight evenly spaced sections around the edge of the circle.

7 With right sides together, match each crease around the circle with a seam in the wreath block. Pin the pieces together, easing the fabric between each of the eight sections. Stitch and press the seam toward the outer edge.

8 Repeat steps 3 through 7 to make three additional blocks. Square up each block to 17 inches (43.2 cm). Arrange them as desired into a two-column grid.

9 Pin two adjacent blocks with right sides together. Stitch along the common side, and press the seam. Repeat with the second pair

of blocks. Pin the sewn pairs with right sides together along the long edges, matching up the seams, and stitch together. Press the seam.

10 Pin and sew the two shorter red border strips to the left and right sides of the quilt top. Pin and sew the remaining longer red strips to the top and bottom. Press all seams. Attach the green border strips to the quilt top in the same way.

11 Make a quilt sandwich with the quilt top, batting, and backing, then pin or baste all layers in place. Quilt as desired (pages 14–15). Trim any excess batting and backing fabric.

12 Stitch the four binding strips together end-to-end to make one long strip, and bind the quilt (pages 15–17).

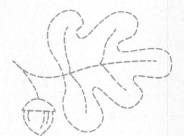

home squash home wall hanging

Cozy up your entryway with a homemade welcome message, great for the autumn months and beyond.

handmade by MONICA SOLORIO-SNOW

fabric & such

Assorted pieces of orange fabric (for the pumpkin), at least 24 inches (61 cm) long

Assorted fabrics in a variety of colors (see chart on page 40)

1 yard (.9 m) of black fabric (for backing and binding)

⅓ yard (.3 m) of white or cream fabric (for appliqué backing)

1 piece of batting, 30 x 42 inches (76.2 x 106.7 cm)

Freezer paper for templates

Embroidery floss

tools

Basic Patchwork Kit (page 9)

Templates (page 122)

finished size

24 x 36 inches (61 x 91.4 cm)

seam allowance

¼ inch (6 mm) unless otherwise indicated. Press all seams to one side, alternating sides where the seams intersect.

notes

• Naturally you can use whatever colors you like, but the cutting instructions use the colors shown in the project for easy identification.

• Yardage for the fabric strips is based on fabric that measures 42 to 44 inches (106.7 to 111.8 cm) wide.

get started

1 Cut the fabrics following the chart below. The recommended approach is to cut strips first (WOF = width of fabric), then cut squares from those strips as listed. (Not all strips will be cut into squares.) Some squares will then need to be cut in half diagonally (from corner to corner).

2 Starting at the top of the quilt, assemble the three star blocks as shown (A), using the pink, yellow, and aqua star pieces and the dark black and medium black squares. Then join the blocks in a row.

3 To make the background for the pumpkin appliqué, stitch the bottom edge of the star row to the top edge of the black strip and the bottom edge of the black strip to the top edge of the gray strip.

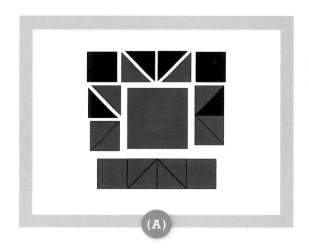

(A)

Press. Continue adding the strips of gray, working your way down from dark to medium to lighter gray to create a slight gradation.

fabric color	strips	squares	notes
Orange (pumpkin)	(5) 6 x 24 inches (15.2 x 61 cm)		
Brown (stem)	(1) 3 x 4 inches (7.6 x 10.2 cm)		
Dark green (leaves)	(1) 5 inches (12.7 cm) x WOF		
Dark black	(1) 2⅞ inches (7.3 cm) x WOF	(6) 2½ inches (6.4 cm)	
		(6) 2⅞ inches (7.3 cm)	cut diagonally
Medium black	(1) 2⅞ inches (7.3 cm) x WOF	(6) 2½ inches (6.4 cm)	
		(6) 2⅞ inches (7.3 cm)	cut diagonally
Light black	(1) 4½ x 24 inches (11.4 x 61 cm)		
Dark gray	(1) 4½ x 24 inches (11.4 x 61 cm)		
Medium gray	(1) 10½ x 24 ½ inches (26.7 x 62.2 cm)		
Light gray	(1) 8½ x 24 ½ inches (21.6 x 62.2 cm)		
Light green (grass)	(1) 2½ x 24 ½ inches (6.4 x 62.2 cm)		
	(1) 5 inches (12.7 cm) x WOF	(6) 5 inches (12.7 cm)	for prairie points
Pink (star)	(1) 4½ inches (11.4 cm) x WOF	(1) 4½ inches (11.4 cm)	
		(4) 2⅞ inches (7.3 cm)	cut diagonally
Yellow (star)	(1) 4½ inches (11.4 cm) x WOF	(1) 4½ inches (11.4 cm)	
		(4) 2⅞ inches (7.3 cm)	cut diagonally
Aqua (star)	(1) 4½ inches (11.4 cm) x WOF	(1) 4½ inches (11.4 cm)	
		(4) 2⅞ inches (7.3 cm)	cut diagonally
Black (backing)	(1) 30 x 42 inches (76.2 x 106.7 cm)		
Black (binding)	(3) 2¼ inches (5.7 cm) x WOF		

4 To appliqué the pumpkin pieces:

- Trace the templates onto the freezer paper's matte side using a pencil. Cut out the shapes along the traced lines.

- Iron the freezer paper pieces, shiny side down, to the wrong side of the pumpkin fabric pieces. Keep in mind you will be working on the reverse sides.

- Trim off any excess fabric about ½ inch (1.3 cm) from the edges of the freezer paper.

- Pin the pieces to the white appliqué backing fabric, with right sides together and the freezer paper on top.

- Stitch completely around the edge of each freezer paper piece, trying not to stitch on top of the freezer paper. Backstitch to lock the beginning and end of the stitches.

- Remove the freezer paper from each piece and trim ¼ inch (6 mm) from the seams. Snip the curves ⅛ inch (3 mm) away from the stitch lines.

- In the center of the white fabric on each piece, carefully cut a 2-inch (5.1 cm) slit for turning. Turn the pieces right side out and press.

- Pin the appliqué pieces in the desired location. Topstitch the pieces in place, as close to the edge as possible. If sewing by hand, you could use a blanket or appliqué stitch (page 13).

5 Create the leaves following the process in step 4.

6 To make the grass section:

- Make six prairie points by folding each light green square diagonally (corner to corner) with wrong sides together, to make a triangle.

Press. Fold the triangle in half to make a smaller triangle, and press again.

- Space the six points along the top edge of the 24½-inch (62.2 cm) light green strip, lining up the raw edges of the prairie points with the raw edge of the strip. Pin in place.

- With right sides facing, pin this strip to the bottom background gray strip and stitch. Press the points up and away from the green strip.

7 Using two strands of floss, embroider "Home Squash Home" and the leaf trails, using the template and the project photograph as your guide.

8 Make a quilt sandwich with the quilt top, batting, and backing, then pin or baste all layers in place. Quilt as desired (pages 14–15). The sample shows hand quilting, echo stitched about ¼ inch (6 mm) around the stars, pumpkin pieces, and leaves, and some free-motion quilting of leaves and leaf trails.

9 Stitch the binding strips together end-to-end to make one long strip and bind the quilt (pages 15–17).

stuffed elves

Little patchwork pants, cute suspenders, and a charming expression make up this sweet pair of elf stuffies. Make one or a gaggle—you can never have too many helping hands at the holidays!

handmade by AMANDA CARESTIO

fabric & such *(to make one)*

2 fat quarters (45.7 x 55.9 cm) of green print fabrics, plus assorted scraps

1 fat quarter (45.7 x 55.9 cm) of red print fabric, plus assorted scraps

1 piece of flesh-toned fabric, 4 inches square (10.2 cm)

1 piece of paper-backed fusible web, 4 inches square (10.2 cm)

Scraps of felt (for hair and button backs)

Embroidery floss

Two red buttons, ½ inch (1.3 cm) in diameter

Polyester fiberfill

tools

Basic Patchwork Kit (page 9)

Templates (page 118)

finished size

Body: 5½ x 11 inches (13.9 x 27.9 cm)

seam allowance

¼ inch (6 mm) unless otherwise indicated

get started

1 Enlarge and cut out the templates. Cut out the following pieces from the fabrics as follows.

For the body:

- 2 template A pieces from green fabric.

- 2 template B pieces from red fabric.

- 1 template C piece from green fabric.

- 1 template D piece from red fabric.

- 1 piece of green fabric measuring 7 x 5 inches (17.8 x 12.7 cm), for the back middle panel.

For the arms:

- 2 pieces of green fabric measuring 4 x 4½ inches (10.2 x 11.4 cm).

- 2 pieces of green fabric, each measuring 2 x 4 inches (5.1 x 10.2 cm), for mittens.

For the legs:

- 2 leg template pieces from green fabric, cut on the fold.

2 For the patchwork (front) pants, cut ten 2-inch (5.1 cm) squares from the red scraps. Stitch together two rows of five squares.

3 To create the middle panel (front torso), pin the two red B pieces on both sides of the green C piece, right sides facing and matching up the long sides. Stitch the pieces together and press. Stitch the pieced pants section from step 2 to the bottom edge (A).

4 To make the face:

- Trace the outline of the face template onto the fusible web and iron the webbing onto the wrong side of the piece of flesh-toned fabric.

- Cut out the face shape, peel off the paper backing, and iron the face onto the center of a green A piece, about ¾ inch (1.9 cm) up from the bottom edge. Sew a zigzag stitch around the shape to secure.

- Trace the hair templates onto the felt and cut them out; stitch them in place on the face. Stitch the rest of the facial features with a backstitch, using an embroidery needle and floss.

5 To assemble the front and back:

- For the front, stitch the face piece to the top edge of the front middle panel.

- For the back, stitch the remaining A piece to the top of the green back middle panel. Stitch the red D piece along the bottom edge (B).

- Use a ruler to even up and trim the side edges.

6 Cut two felt circles that are somewhat larger than the buttons. Layer each felt circle under a button and stitch them to the bottom of the elf front B pieces (these are the meant to be fasteners for the "suspenders"). Position the buttons as far in from the outside edge as possible to allow for the side seams.

7 To make the arms:

- Stitch a mitten piece to an arm piece along a 4-inch (10.2 cm) edge.

- Fold the arm in half lengthwise, with right sides facing, and stitch across the mitten end and down one side (C). Clip the corner.

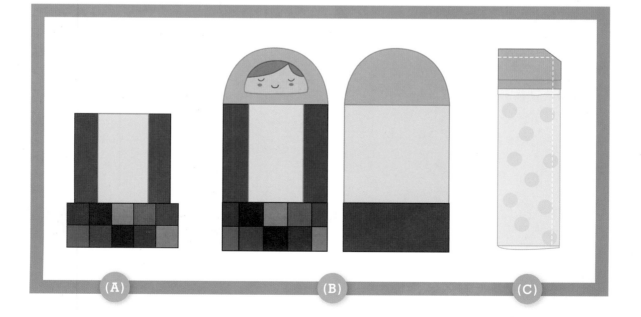

(A) (B) (C)

- Turn right side out and stuff with the polyester fiberfill.

- Repeat to make the other arm.

8 To make the legs:

- Fold a leg in half lengthwise, with right sides facing, and stitch along the long edge, around the toe, and around the bottom of the foot. Clip the curves.

- Turn right side out, and stuff with the polyester fiberfill.

- Repeat to make the other leg.

9 To assemble the doll:

- Lay the front panel right side up on your work surface.

- Pin the left arm in place on the left side, just below the seam between the face A piece and the middle panel, lining up the raw edges.

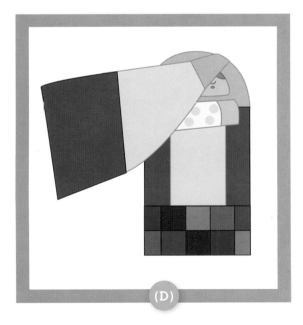

(D)

- Lay the back panel on top and stitch the side edge over the arm **(D)** and around the A piece.

- Attach the right arm in the same way, pinning the front and back panels together and stitching over the right arm.

- Continue working your way around the doll, adding the legs at the bottom. Be sure to leave a 3-inch (7.6 cm) opening along one side for turning.

10 Turn the doll right side out, stuff with polyester fiberfill, and whipstitch the opening closed. You're done!

insulated
buffet runner

Replace your regular batting with insulated batting for a runner that is not only beautiful to look at but highly functional as well.

handmade by **MARILYN BUTLER**

fabric & such

5 fat quarters (45.7 x 55.9 cm) in
   assorted colors

½ yard (.5 m) of tan printed fabric
   (for background and binding)

½ yard (.5 m) of coordinating fabric
   (for backing)

1 piece of cotton batting, 18 x 45 inches
   (45.7 x 114.3 cm)

1 piece of insulated batting, 18 x 45 inches
   (45.7 x 114.3 cm)

tools

Basic Patchwork Kit (page 9)

finished size

14 x 42 inches (35.6 x 106.7 cm)

seam allowance

¼ inch (6 mm); press seams open
   to reduce bulk.

get started

1 Cut out the following pieces from the assorted fat quarters.

- 11 strips, each measuring 14½ x 2½ inches (35.6 x 6.4 cm).

- 10 strips, each measuring 4½ x 2½ inches (11.4 x 6.4 cm).

2 Cut out the following pieces from the tan fabric:

- 10 strips for the background, each measuring 10½ x 2½ inches (26.7 x 6.4 cm).

- 3 strips for binding, each measuring 2½ inches (6.4 cm) x the width of the fabric.

3 Stitch each of the tan background strips to the assorted 4½-inch (11.4 cm) fat quarter strips, end-to-end, to make a total of 10 strips that measure 14½ inches (35.6 cm) long.

4 Lay out the strips in placement order, using the project photo as a guide. Alternate fat quarter strips with pieced strips as desired.

5 Starting at one end of the runner, pin a pieced strip to a fat quarter strip, right sides together, and stitch along the common side. Press the seam open. Repeat with the remaining strips in order until all of the strips are attached. Press.

6 Make a quilt sandwich with the runner top, cotton batting, insulated batting, and backing, then pin or baste all layers in place. Quilt ¼ inch (6 mm) on both sides of each long seam, using a walking foot (if you have one).

7 Stitch the three binding strips together end-to-end to make one long strip and bind the table runner (pages 15–17).

countdown-to-christmas advent calendar

Linen and hand-stamped numbers give the advent calendar project a casual, worn-in feel that makes it seem like it's been part of the family for years.

handmade by KAYE PRINCE

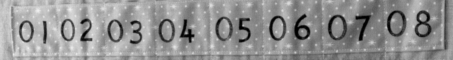

fabric & such

Assorted green fabric scraps for the tree and border, enough for four 3 x 15-inch (7.6 x 38.1 cm) strips

Assorted green fabrics for pocket strips, enough for three 2½ x 16½-inch (6.4 x 41.9 cm) strips

Brown fabric scrap for the tree trunk

½ yard (.5 m) of linen (for background and binding), 54 inches (137.2 cm) wide

½ yard (.5 m) of backing fabric

½ yard (.5 m) of batting

tools

Basic Patchwork Kit (page 9)

Template (page 120)

Numeric rubber stamps, ¾ inch (1.9 cm) in diameter

Ink pad suitable for fabric

finished size

12½ x 30½ inches (31.8 x 77.5 cm)

seam allowance

¼ inch (6 mm) unless otherwise indicated; press all seams open.

get started

1 Copy and cut out 11 hexagon templates. Set aside.

2 Cut out the following pieces from the fabrics.

From the linen fabric:

- 2 binding strips, each measuring 2 inches (5.1 cm) x the width of the fabric.

- 1 rectangle measuring 9½ x 10½ inches (24.1 x 26.7 cm).

- 1 rectangle measuring 10½ x 18½ inches (26.7 x 47 cm).

From assorted green fabrics:

- 10 squares for the tree, each measuring 2½ inches (6.4 cm).

- 3 strips for the pocket strips, each measuring 2½ x 16½ inches (6.4 x 41.9 cm).

- 4 strips for the hanging tabs, each measuring 1¼ x 2½ inches (3.2 x 6.4 cm).

- 12 strips for the border from four coordinating green fabrics, each measuring 1½ x 2½ inches (3.8 x 6.4 cm), for a total of 46 strips. (You will use 45.)

From the brown fabric scrap:

- 1 square measuring 2½ inches (6.4 cm).

3 To make the hexagon tree:

- Follow the instructions on page 12 to paper-piece 10 green hexagons for the tree and one brown hexagon for the trunk. Do not remove the paper templates from the hexagons.

- Lay out the tree shape so you can see which hexagon sides meet. Beginning from the top, whipstitch together two adjacent hexagons along the meeting edges, right sides together, making sure not to catch the template paper. Stitch all the hexagons together.

- Remove the paper templates from the hexagons.

- Lay out the 9½ x 10½-inch (24.1 x 26.7 cm) piece of linen with the long sides running vertically. Center and pin the hexagon tree onto the linen piece.

- Using a ¹⁄₁₆-inch (1.6 mm) seam allowance, topstitch all the way around the edges of the tree.

4 To make the main body and borders:

- Stitch together five border strips, end-to-end, in an A-B-C-D-A pattern.

- With right sides facing, stitch this strip to the right-hand side of the linen hexagon tree piece.

- With right sides facing, stitch the remaining linen rectangle to the right-hand side of the border strip. This piece now forms the main body of the calendar.

- Stitch together the remaining border strips, end-to-end, in a repeating A-B-C-D pattern, using 15 rectangles for each top and bottom border, and five for each side border.

- Beginning with the short borders, attach these strips to the main body of the calendar.

5 To make the advent pockets:

- For each pocket strip, press under all four edges ¼ inch (6 mm) toward the wrong side of the fabric. Topstitch one long folded edge to form the top edge of each pocket. Each pocket strip should now measure 2 x 16 inches (5.1 x 40.6 cm).

- Use a disappearing fabric marker to mark eight 2-inch squares (5.1 cm) along the width of each pocket strip.

- Following the manufacturer's instructions, center and stamp each square with numbers from 01 to 24, in sequential order across the three pocket pieces using the rubber stamps and ink pad.

- Once the ink has dried, arrange and pin the pocket pieces evenly on the calendar side of the linen, leaving 1 inch (2.5 cm) around each side of the pocket pieces.

- Topstitch ⅛ inch (3 mm) from the edge along three sides of each pocket, leaving the top edge open.

- To divide each strip into numbered pockets, stitch along the marked lines, straight down from the top of the first pocket strip to the bottom of the third pocket strip, backstitching to lock the beginning and end of the stitches.

6 Make a quilt sandwich with the calendar top, batting, and backing, and quilt as desired, making sure not to quilt over the hexagon tree or the pockets.

7 To make the hanging tabs:

- Fold each hanging tab strip in half with right sides together and long sides meeting. Stitch along the long sides and trim the seam allowances to ⅛ inch (3 mm). Turn each tab right side out and press.

- Fold each tab in half to form a loop. Evenly space the four hanging tabs on the back of the calendar along the top edge; place a tab close to each corner but not close enough to interfere with the binding. Abut the raw edges of each loop to the raw edge of the calendar (the loop will be pointing down) and stitch in place with a ⅛-inch (3 mm) seam.

8 Stitch the two linen binding strips together end-to-end to make one long strip. Use your preferred method to make and attach double-fold binding (pages 15–17).

The Quite Personable Pickle Ornament

Based on the lovably odd tradition in which a pickle-shaped ornament is hidden deep within the Christmas tree and the first child to find it is blessed with a year of good fortune (and an extra gift), this pickle is sure to be a crowd pleaser!

handmade by **JOHN Q. ADAMS**

fabric & such

1 piece of green wool felt, 11 x 17 inches (27.9 x 43.2 cm)

Embroidery floss in green and black, 36 inches (91.4 cm) long

Ribbon scrap

Polyester fiberfill

Cardboard for template, 4 x 8 inches (10.2 x 20.3 cm)

tools

Basic Patchwork Kit (page 9)

Template (118)

get started

1 Trace the pickle template onto the cardboard and cut out the shape. Trace the template onto the felt. Flip over the template and trace it onto the felt a second time (to make a mirror image of the first).

2 Embroider a face onto one of the pickle shapes, adding two French knots for the eyes and a simple backstitch for the mouth, using an embroidery needle and black floss. Using green floss, stitch a running stitch to create the texture of your pickle on both pickle shapes **(A)**.

Tip: Use the side of the felt with the template tracing as the wrong side of your embroidery.

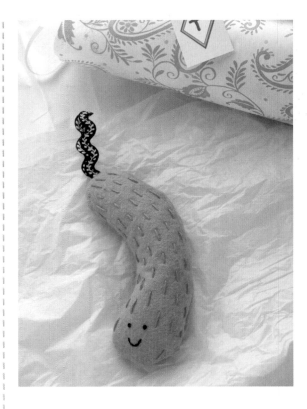

3 Cut out both pieces approximately ¼ inch (6 mm) from your traced line.

4 Cut a small piece of ribbon, fold it into a loop, and place it along the top edge of your pickle front with the loop facing inward, toward the center of the pickle body.

5 Pin the back piece of your pickle on top of the front, with right sides facing. Stitch around your pickle ornament using your traced line as a guide, leaving a 3 to 4–inch (7.6 to 10.2 cm) opening between the start and end of your seam for turning. Backstitch to lock the beginning and end of the stitches.

6 Turn the ornament right side out through the opening, pushing out along the seams to smooth the edges of your ornament. The ribbon loop should stick out from the top of the ornament for hanging.

7 Insert the polyester fiberfill through the opening of the pickle, and hand stitch the opening closed.

hedgehog holidays patchwork pillowcase and stuffed toy

This precious pillowcase combines an embroidered hedgehog with a pretty patchwork trim, perfect for dressing your guest bed for holiday visitors. Add a matching stuffed hedgehog, and your guests may never leave!

handmade by NICOLE VOS VAN AVEZATHE

fabric & such

FOR THE PILLOWCASE

1⅓ yard (1.2 m) of white fabric

Assorted red and green fabric scraps, at least 4½ inches square (11.4 cm)

Embroidery floss

Four or more matching trims

FOR THE HEDGEHOG

2 pieces of brown felt (for the body), 6½ inches square (16.5 cm)

Felt scraps for face, snout, mittens, and apple

Scrap of fabric (for the legs)

Embroidery floss

Polyester fiberfill

tools

Basic Patchwork Kit (page 9)

Templates (page 118)

finished size

Pillowcase: 28 x 18¾ inches (71.1 cm x 47.6 cm)

seam allowance

¼ inch (6 mm) unless otherwise indicated

get started

the pillowcase

1 Cut out the following pieces from the white fabric:

- 1 piece for the left front: 20½ x 19½ inches (52.1 x 49.5 cm).

- 1 piece for the right front: 5 x 19½ inches (12.7 x 49.5 cm).

- 1 piece for the back: 38 x 19½ inches (96.5 x 49.5 cm).

- 1 piece for the embroidery: 6½ x 4½ inches (16.5 x 11.4 cm).

2 From the red and green scraps, cut strips that measure 4½ inches (11.4 cm) wide and vary in height from 2 to 4 inches (5.7 to 10.2 cm). Depending on the height of the strips, you will need five to seven different fabrics.

3 Transfer the hedgehog stitch template to the 6½ x 4½–inch (16.5 x 11.4 cm) piece of white fabric. Embroider as desired using an embroidery needle and floss. The sample shown was sewn primarily with backstitches and straight stitches (page 13).

4 To make the patchwork band on the front:

- Arrange the colored strips in a pleasing layout, varying the prints and colors. Stitch the strips together along the 4½-inch (11.4 cm) edges until the pieced strip measures at least 13½ inches (34.3 cm) long.

- Sew the embroidered hedgehog panel to the top of the pieced strip.

- Embellish with trims as desired, topstitching 5-inch (12.7 cm) lengths over the tops of some of the patchwork seams.

5 To assemble the pillowcase:

- On one short edge of the right front piece, make a ½-inch (1.3 cm) double-fold hem. Hem one short edge of the pillowcase back in the same way.

- With right sides facing, stitch the long raw edge of the right front piece to the right side of the patchwork strip. In the same way, stitch the left front piece to the left side of the patchwork strip. Press all seams flat.

- Fold the hemmed edge of the back piece 7 inches (17.8 cm) to the wrong side and adjust as needed to match the size of the top piece. Press a crease along the folded edge.

- With right sides together, stitch the front to the back, leaving open the hemmed side. Your festive pillowcase is finished!

the hedgehog stuffy

1 Enlarge and cut out the templates. Cut out the shapes from the felt as indicated in the materials list, and cut the legs from the fabric scrap.

2 Position the snout on the face, and then stitch in place. Embroider French knots (page 13) for the eyes and nose using an embroidery needle and floss.

3 Place the face/snout on the front body piece, about ¾ inch (1.9 cm) below the top edge to allow for the seam. Fold the ears slightly and tuck the lower part of the ears behind the face. Stitch carefully around the face shape, securing the ears, but stop about 2 inches (5.1 cm) short of completing the seam. Push a bit of the polyester fiberfill behind the face, then finish stitching the face to the body.

4 Position the mittens on the front body, leaving room for seam allowance. Stitch in place. The front of the hedgehog is now complete.

5 Using an embroidery needle and floss, embroider the quills on the hedgehog's back with a running stitch, again leaving room for the seam allowance. Position the apple wherever you like and stitch in place.

6 Pin two leg pieces with right sides together and stitch around the sides and bottom, leaving the top edge open. Turn the legs right side out and stuff with a little bit of polyester fiberfill. Baste the legs closed.

7 Pin the legs onto the front with the raw ends of the legs overlapping the bottom edge of the felt (legs will be on top of the body). With right sides facing, pin the back piece onto the front piece, tucking in the ears and legs. Stitch around the outside edge, leaving a 2-inch (5.1 cm) opening on one side.

8 Turn the hedgehog right side out and stuff with polyester fiberfill. Stitch the opening closed.

fun fun holiday bunting

Amp up your festivities with this super fun patchwork bunting, perfect for scrap busting and totally customizable!

handmade by **JENI BAKER**

fabric & such

⅛ yard (.15 m) each of seven red print fabrics

¾ yard (.7 m) of white cotton fabric (for letters and binding)

¾ yard (.7 m) of backing fabric

tools

Basic Patchwork Kit (page 9)

14 plastic bags

finished size

7 inches square (17.8 cm) for each finished letter

seam allowance

¼ inch (6 mm) unless otherwise indicated

get started

1 Cut the following pieces from the fabrics using a rotary cutter.

- From each of the seven print fabrics: 2 strips, each measuring 1½ inches (3.8 cm) x the width of the fabric. You will have 14 strips that measure 44 inches (111.8 cm) long. Trim the selvedge off each end of the strips.

- From the white fabric: 7 strips the same width and length as the print strips. Trim the selvedges in the same way as before.

- Use the following chart to cut the required number of pieces from each strip. All strips are 1½ inches (3.8 cm) wide, so the numbers refer to the length. After cutting each piece, make sure to keep each size separate.

length of strip	red	white
1½ inches (3.8 cm)	132	90
2½ inches (6.4 cm)	9	6
3½ inches (8.9 cm)	33	7
4½ inches (11.4 cm)	7	2
5½ inches (14 cm)	4	13
7½ inches (19 cm)	28	0

2 From the white fabric, cut the following strips for binding, then trim off selvedges in the same way as before.

- 4 strips, each measuring 2 inches (5.1 cm) x the width of the fabric.

- 1 strip that measures 2 x 21 inches (5.1 x 53.3 cm).

3 From the backing fabric, cut 14 squares measuring 7½ inches (19 cm).

4 Organize the cut pieces for each letter as follows:

- Using office paper, cut out 14 rectangles, labeling each with a letter in Merry Christmas. Place one letter in each plastic bag.

- Starting with the letter M, refer to the Letter Table (page 124) to select the correct fabric pieces needed for each letter and place them in the corresponding bag. Be sure to choose a variety of prints for each letter.

- Continue until you've finished creating little kits for each letter.

5 Stitch the pieces for each letter together, one at a time, using the following instructions:

- Starting with the letter M, lay out all of the pieces according to the diagram provided (A). Double-check it before you start sewing!

- Stitch each column to make seven pieced strips that measure 7½ x 1½ inches

(19 x 3.8 cm). Press the seams to one side, alternating the direction every other column.

- Sew the seven pieced columns together, resulting in a completed letter. Press seams open.

- Square up the block to 7½ inches square (19 cm).

- Continue until you've finished sewing each letter.

6 Pair up each letter with a backing square and pin them together, right sides facing. Leaving the top open, stitch around the sides and the bottom, backstitching to lock the beginning and end of the stitches. Continue until you've finished sewing each letter flag.

7 Carefully clip the corners on each flag. Turn them right side out, using a turning tool to gently push out the corners. Press.

8 Stitch the five binding strips together end-to-end to make one long strip. Fold the two short raw ends to the wrong side ½ inch (1.3 cm) and press. Topstitch in place. Fold the strip into double-fold binding (pages 15–17). The finished length should be 186 inches (472.4 cm).

9 Put the letter flags in order and assemble the bunting as follows:

- Measure and mark the inside of the binding tape 30 inches (76.2 cm) from one end, using a disappearing fabric marker.

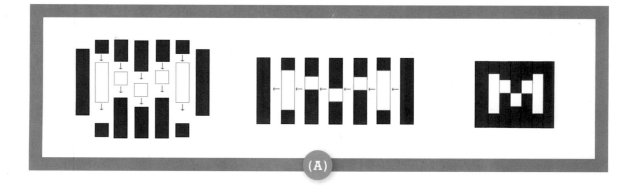

(A)

- Tuck the first flag (letter M) into the folds of the binding, lining up the left edge of the flag with the mark you just made. Pin in place.

- Measure and mark the binding 2 inches (5.1 cm) from the right edge of this flag. Insert the second letter, lining up the left edge with the new mark. Continue assembling the flags in the same way, leaving a 4-inch (10.2 cm) space between the words Merry and Christmas.

10 Topstitch along the open edge of the binding, ⅛ inch (3 mm) from the edge, catching the bunting flags as you go. Backstitch to lock the beginning and end of the stitches. Trim the threads, remove pins, press, and enjoy!

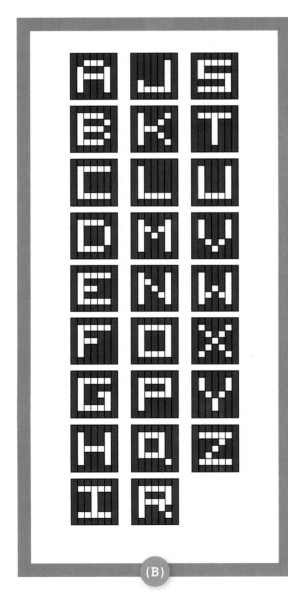

(B)

letter table

All 26 letters of the alphabet are included here for you to easily customize this project. Refer to (B) and the chart on page 124 for cutting lists for each of the letters. To estimate yardage needed for your customized bunting, select your letters and add up the total strip length provided for each letter. Divide your total number by 42. This will give you the number of 1½ x 42–inch (3.8 cm x 106.7 cm) strips you'll need. Multiply that number by 1½ inches (3.8 cm) to get the yardage needed in inches (centimeters). Once again, the numbers represent the length of the strips.

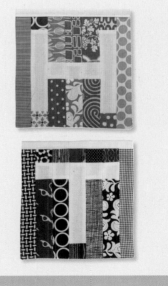

modern heirloom quilt

This instant family heirloom has a traditional flair with a decidedly modern design, pairing traditional holiday hues of red and green with generous negative space.

handmade by **JOHN Q. ADAMS**

fabric & such

14 fat quarters (45.7 x 55.9 cm) in assorted red and green prints

2¼ yards (2.1 m) of green fabric

2¼ yards (2.1 m) of white fabric

5½ yards (5 m) of backing fabric

Double sized batting

½ yard (.5 m) of binding fabric

tools

Basic Patchwork Kit (page 9)

finished size

70 x 80 inches (177.8 x 203.2 cm)

seam allowance

¼ inch (6 mm) unless otherwise indicated

get started

1 Cut the following pieces from the fabrics. (For the improv-style log cabin quilt blocks, you'll cut as you piece.)

- From solid green fabric: 1 piece measuring 22½ x 80 inches (57.2 x 203.2 cm)

- From solid white fabric: 1 piece measuring 16½ x 80 inches (41.9 x 203.2 cm)

- From binding fabric: 7 strips, each measuring 2½ x 44 inches (6.4 x 111.8 cm). Trim the selvedges from the binding strips.

2 Study the assembly diagram for the quilt (A). Consider the layout when planning color and fabric placement for your blocks. You will be making a total of:

- 3 of block 1

- 4 of block 2

- 3 of block 3

All quilt blocks are 12½ inches square (31.8 cm) before adding frames, and 16½ inches square (41.9 cm) once frames are added.

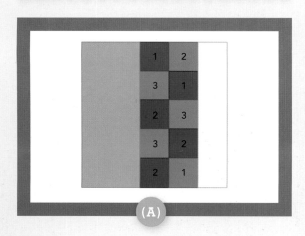

(A)

3 Make three of block 1 (B), cutting the fabric as you piece:

- As shown in the diagram, begin with a 2½-inch (6.4 cm) center square (piece 1) cut from a printed fabric.

- Stitch a 2½-inch (6.4 cm) square (piece 2) to the right side of the center square. Press.

- Stitch a 2½ x 4½–inch (6.4 x 11.4 cm) rectangle (piece 3) to the top of the pieced squares. Press.

- Continue adding pieces in a counter-clockwise fashion, following the measurements in the chart. Note that pieces 13 through 15 can be stitched together before joining these pieces to the quilt block.

- Once the quilt block is complete, add a uniform 2½-inch (6.4 cm) "frame" around the block (F1–F4).

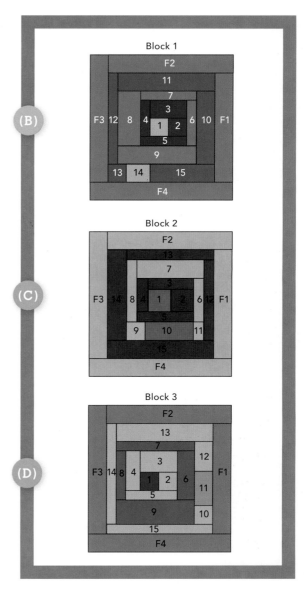

Block 1

Block 2

Block 3

piece	size
1	2½ inches square (6.4 cm)
2	2½ inches square (6.4 cm)
3	2½ x 4½ inches (6.4 x 11.4 cm)
4	1½ x 4½ inches (3.8 x 11.4 cm)
5	1½ x 5½ inches (3.8 x 14 cm)
6	1½ x 5½ inches (3.8 x 14 cm)
7	1½ x 6½ inches (3.8 x 16.5 cm)
8	3½ x 6½ inches (8.9 x 16.5 cm)
9	2½ x 9½ inches (6.4 x 24.1 cm)
10	2½ x 8½ inches (6.4 x 21.6 cm)
11	2½ x 11½ inches (6.4 x 29.2 cm)
12	1½ x 10½ inches (3.8 x 26.7 cm)
13	2½ inches square (6.4 cm)
13	2½ inches square (6.4 cm)
14	2½ x 3½ inches (6.4 x 8.9 cm)
15	2½ x 7½ inches (6.4 x 19 cm)
F1	2½ x 12½ inches (6.4 x 31.8 cm)
F2	2½ x 14½ inches (6.4 x 36.8 cm)
F3	2½ x 14½ inches (6.4 x 36.8 cm)
F4	2½ x 16½ inches (6.4 x 41.9 cm)

4 Make four of block 2 (C):

- Begin in the center as before and construct the block in a counter-clockwise fashion, following the measurements in the chart.

- Note that pieces 9 through 11 can be stitched together before joining these pieces to the quilt block.

- Add a uniform frame around the block as before.

piece	size
1	3½ inches square (8.9 cm)
2	3½ inches square (8.9 cm)
3	1½ x 6½ inches (3.8 x 16.5 cm)
4	1½ x 4½ inches (3.8 x 11.4 cm)
5	1½ x 7½ inches (3.8 x 19 cm)
6	1½ x 5½ inches (3.8 x 14 cm)
7	2½ x 8½ inches (6.4 x 21.6 cm)
8	1½ x 7½ inches (3.8 x 19 cm)
9	2½ inches square (6.4 cm)
10	2½ x 6½ inches (6.4 x 16.5 cm)
11	2½ x 1½ inches (6.4 x 3.8 cm)
12	1½ x 9½ inches (3.8 x 24.1 cm)
13	1½ x 10½ inches (3.8 x 26.7 cm)
14	2½ x 10½ inches (6.4 x 26.7 cm)
15	2½ x 12½ inches (6.4 x 31.8 cm)
F1	2½ x 12½ inches (6.4 x 31.8 cm)
F2	2½ x 14½ inches (6.4 x 36.8 cm)
F3	2 ½ x 14½ inches (6.4 x 36.8 cm)
F4	2½ x 16½ inches (6.4 x 41.9 cm)

piece	size
12	2½ x 3½ inches (6.4 x 8.9 cm)
13	2½ x 11½ inches (6.4 x 29.2 cm)
14	1½ x 11½ inches (3.8 x 29.2 cm)
15	1½ x 12½ inches (3.8 x 31.8 cm)
F1	2½ x 12½ inches (6.4 x 31.8 cm)
F2	2½ x 14½ inches (6.4 x 36.8 cm)
F3	2½ x 14½ inches (6.4 x 36.8 cm)
F4	2½ x 16½ inches (6.4 x 41.9 cm)

6 Assemble the quilt top:

- Referring to (A), lay out the quilt blocks, alternating the dominant colors. Rotate the blocks in any way you wish until you achieve an eye-pleasing layout. Stitch them together into a column.

- Attach the green panel to the left side of the pieced column and the white panel to the right side. Press seams toward the solid color panels.

7 Make a quilt sandwich with the quilt top, batting, and backing fabric. Baste all layers together and quilt them by machine or hand. Trim any excess batting and backing fabric.

8 Stitch the binding strips together end-to-end to make one long strip and bind the quilt (pages 15–17).

5 Make three of block 3 (D):

- Begin in the center as before and construct the block in a counter-clockwise fashion, following the measurements in the chart.

- Note that pieces 10 through 12 can be stitched together before joining these pieces to the quilt block.

- Add a uniform frame around the block as before.

piece	size
1	2½ inches square (6.4 cm)
2	2½ inches square (6.4 cm)
3	2½ x 4½ inches (6.4 x 11.4 cm)
4	2½ x 4½ inches (6.4 x 11.4 cm)
5	1½ x 6 ½inches (3.8 x 16.5 cm)
6	2½ x 5½ inches (6.4 x 14 cm)
7	1½ x 8½ inches (3.8 x 21.6 cm)
8	1½ x 6½ inches (3.8 x 3.8 cm)
9	3½ x 9½ inches (8.9 x 24.1 cm)
10	2½ inches square (6.4 cm)
11	2½ x 4½ inches (6.4 x 11.4 cm)

trees all around tree skirt

The simple, graphic tree design and effective use of solid fabrics gives modern appeal to this tree skirt.

handmade by **CHARLIE SCOTT AND RYAN WALSH FOR PATCHWORK SQUARED**

fabric & such

1 bright solid color charm pack that includes 17 green fabrics

1 bright solid color jelly roll

¼ yard (.2 m) of brown fabric (for tree trunks)

½ yard (.5 m) of gray fabric (for background)

⅓ yard (.34 m) of gray fabric (for sashing)

½ yard (.5 m) of red fabric (for binding)

1 piece of backing fabric, 34 inches square (86.4 cm)

1 piece of batting, 34 inches square (86.4 cm)

tools

Basic Patchwork Kit (page 9)

Templates (page 119)

Round object for tracing, 5 inches (12.7 cm) in diameter

finished size

32 inches square (81.3 cm)

seam allowance

Scant ¼ inch (6 mm) unless otherwise indicated

note

For this project, choose a charm pack that includes 42 scraps of fabric, 5 inches square (12.7 cm), and a jelly roll containing 40 strips of fabric, each measuring 12½ x 44 inches (6.4 x 111.8 cm). These bundled packs of fabrics can be found at many fabric and quilting stores and online.

get started

1 Enlarge and cut out the templates, then cut out the following pieces from the fabrics.

From the green charm fabrics: 68 template C pieces. You can cut four C pieces from each 5-inch square (12.7 cm) charm.

From background fabric:

- 68 rectangles, each measuring 3 x 6 inches (7.6 x 15.2 cm). Using templates A and B, cut the rectangles into triangles.

- Two strips, each measuring 1¼ inches (3.2 cm) x the width of the fabric.

From brown fabric:

- 1 strip measuring 1 inch (2.5 cm) x the width of the fabric.

2 To create the trees:

- Sew a background triangle A piece and a background triangle B piece to the left and right edge of each green tree triangle C piece. Set seams and press the seams toward the tree pieces. You'll need 68 total A-C-B (tree) pieces, each measuring 2½ inches square (6.4 cm).

- Using a scant ¼-inch (6 mm) seam allowance, sew the background strips to the sides of the brown (tree trunk) strip. Cut the pieced strip into sixty-eight 1½-inch (3.8 cm) segments. Press the seams toward the trunk.

- Stitch one tree trunk segment to the bottom of one tree piece, with right sides together (A). Press the seams open. Repeat this process for the remaining trees, 68 tree blocks total.

3 Sew the jelly roll strips along the left edge and across the top edge of 16 tree blocks, as you would in creating a log cabin block (page 11). You'll need four shades of each solid color to create the log cabins as shown (B). Create four log cabin blocks for each section in each color-way, with each block measuring 6½ inches square (16.5 cm). You will need 16 total log cabin blocks.

4 Using the project photograph as a guide, sew four of the same color log cabin blocks together to make one large block that measures 12½ inches (31.8 cm) unfinished. Remember to turn each block 90°, so that your trees form a square in the middle. Repeat to make one large block for each color.

5 Cut out the following pieces from the fabrics.

From the gray sashing fabric:

- 2 strips, each measuring 24½ x 1½ inches (62.2 x 3.8 cm).

- 2 strips, each measuring 26½ x 1½ inches (67.3 x 3.8 cm).

From the gray background fabric:

- 4 squares, each measuring 3½ inches (8.9 cm).

- 1 rectangle measuring 2½ x 3½ inches (6.4 x 8.9 cm).

From the red binding fabric: 4 strips, each measuring 2¼ inches (5.7 cm) x the width of the fabric. Set aside.

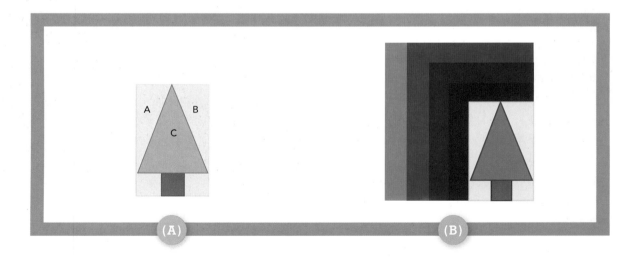

(A)   (B)

6 Stitch the four log cabin tree blocks together. Sew the sashing strips cut in step 5 around the edges of this joined center block as follows:

- Sew the 24½-inch (62.2 cm) strips to the left and right sides of the center block.

- Press the seams toward the side strips.

- Sew the 26½-inch (67.3 cm) strips to the top and bottom sides of the center block.

- Press the seams toward the top and bottom strips. The center block should measure 26½ inches square (67.3 cm).

7 Join six tree blocks together, alternating directions. Repeat to make two strips. Sew the strips together end-to-end, with the 2½ x 3½-inch (6.4 x 8.9 cm) rectangle of background fabric cut in step 5 in the middle. Sew the strip to one side of the center block. Press the seams toward the center block.

8 Join 13 tree blocks together, alternating directions, to form a strip that measures 26½ inches (67.3 cm) long. Repeat to make three total strips.

9 Sew one of the strips with 13 trees to the other side of the center block (opposite the strip you added in step 7). Press the seams toward the center border.

10 Sew a 3½-inch (8.9 cm) background fabric square to each end of the two remaining strips. Sew these strips to the top and bottom of the center block. Press the seams toward the center border. Your center block should measure 32 inches square (81.3 cm) at this point.

11 Make a quilt sandwich with the quilt top, batting, and backing, and quilt as desired (pages 14–15).

12 Center the round tracing object on your quilt top and trace around it using a disappearing fabric marker.

13 Cut a slit in the quilt, cutting through the middle of the plain background square on the outside edge and along the outside edges of the log cabin blocks. Continue cutting out the outline of the circle so that you have the opening in the skirt for the tree.

14 Bind the quilt using the red binding strips cut in step 5 as follows: up one side of the slit, along the outside edges, and along the other side of the slit. Then lay your binding strips around the circle opening and make sure the strips extend evenly on both sides. You will need about 56 inches (142.2 cm) of binding for the opening (with enough left over to make a tie for your skirt). Start by sewing closed one end of the tie, binding the raw edges around the circle opening, and sewing closed the other end of the tie.

harvest vine table runner

This project looks like it came straight out of a design catalog, yet it is surprisingly easy to make and easy to customize for many holidays throughout the year.

handmade by **JESSICA KOVACH**

get started

1 Enlarge and cut out templates A and B. Cut out the following pieces from the fabrics.

From the background fabric:

- 1 strip measuring 4½ inches (11.4 cm) x the width of the fabric; cut this strip into twelve 3½-inch (8.9 cm) sections. Trace template B onto each section twice (A). Cut out all 24 B pieces.

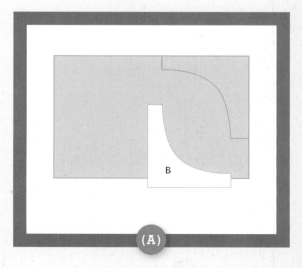

(A)

- 3 strips, each measuring 1¼ inches (3.2 cm) x the width of the fabric, for sashing. Cut these strips into fourteen 6½-inch (16.5 cm) pieces.

- 5 strips measuring 2½ inches (6.4 cm) x the width of the fabric. Two strips will be used for the outside border of the quilt top and three will be used for the binding.

From each of the six print fabrics:

- 4 squares, each measuring 3½ inches (8.9 cm).

- 4 template A pieces.

From dark brown fabric: 1 strip measuring 1½ inches (3.8 cm) x the width of the fabric.

2 Make the pieced leaf blocks:

- Gather eight pieces cut from the same print (four squares and four template A pieces) and four template B pieces. Set aside the four squares for now.

- Fold each piece, one at a time, along its curved edge and finger-press a crease to mark the center point of that edge.

- Pin each A piece to a B piece with right sides together, matching up the center points (B).

- Pin the ends together and ease the rest of the fabric in between the pins. (C).

Tip: *Make ⅛-inch (3 mm) snips along the curved edges of the B pieces to help ease the fabric.*

- Stitch the seam and press the seam allowance toward the background fabric.

- Repeat to make four pieced blocks for each set of leaves; there are six leaves in the sample.

3 Complete the leaf blocks:

- Lay out the leaves by pairing up the four pieced squares with the four matching squares set aside in step 2 (D).

- With right sides facing, stitch the top two squares together and press. Stitch the bottom two squares together in the same way.

- Stitch the top and bottom sections together to form one four-patch leaf block.

- Stitch together all six sets of leaves.

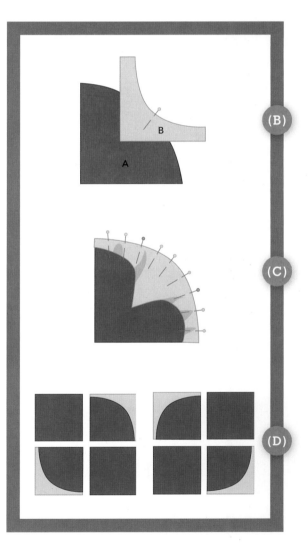

4 Lay out the completed leaf blocks in your desired order, with a sashing strip above and below each one. Stitch the sashing to the leaf blocks, making two long leaf sections. Press seams toward the sashing.

5 Lay out the two leaf sections on the sides of the center stem. Stitch the stem piece in place, making sure to align the leaf sections on opposite sides of the stem. Press seams toward the stem.

6 Pin and stitch the two outside border strips onto the left and right sides of the pieced leaves. Press seams toward the outside border. Trim the ends of the stem and outside borders to square up your quilt top.

7 Make a quilt sandwich with the quilt top, batting, and backing, and quilt as desired. Trim excess batting and backing fabric.

8 Stitch the three binding strips together end-to-end to form one long strip. Fold and press the binding strip in half and attach as a double-fold binding (pages 15–17).

color play!

Create your leaves in different colorways to tailor this table runner to a variety of holidays and seasons. You could try red and green for a traditional Christmas combination, or make the leaves in bright green shades to celebrate spring.

milk & cookie mats

Make the memories even more special for you and your family by making these homemade mini-placemats, perfect for holding a few cookies and a cold glass of milk. Oh, and my children implore you: PLEASE leave a few carrots for the reindeer. They get hungry too, you know.

handmade by JOHN Q. ADAMS

fabric & such

FOR THE TREE

Assorted pieces of green and brown fabric (for tree and trunk), each 4 to 5 inches square (10.2 to 12.7 cm)

6 pieces of linen, each 5 x 6 inches (12.7 x 15.2 cm)

1 piece of backing fabric, 13 x 14 inches (33 x 35.6 cm)

1 strip of binding fabric (or 1 jelly roll strip), 2½ x 44 inches (6.4 x 111.8 cm)

1 piece of batting, 13 x 14 inches (33 x 35.6 cm)

1 piece of cardstock (for the template), 5 inches square (12.7 cm)

FOR THE CIRCLE

5 strips of fabric, 2½ x 10 inches (6.4 x 25.4 cm)

2 pieces of fabric (for background and backing), 10 inches square (25.4 cm)

1 piece of batting, at least 10 inches square (25.4 cm)

Cardstock for template

Aluminum foil

tools

Basic Patchwork Kit (page 9)

Templates (page 120)

Plate or other round object for tracing, 7½ inches (19 cm) in diameter

finished size

Tree: 7 x 9⅗ inches (17.6 x 24.5 cm)

Circle: 9⅗ x 9⅘ inches (24.5 x 25 cm)

seam allowance

¼ inch (6 mm) unless otherwise indicated

get started

the tree

1 Trace the triangle template onto the cardstock and cut out the shape.

2 Cut three 5-inch squares (12.7 cm) of green fabric.

3 Stack your three squares and lay the cardstock triangle template on top of the stack, aligning the bottom edge of your template with the bottom edge of your fabric. Cut along the edges of your template, creating three triangles from your green fabric.

4 Set aside one triangle for your treetop. Trim off the tops of the other two triangles so they each measure 2½ inches (6.4 cm) tall from the bottom edge.

5 Using your triangle template, cut one end off one piece of linen at an angle matching the shape of your triangle. Repeat with another piece of linen. Lay your full triangle in between the two pieces of cut linen.

6 Cut two of the remaining linen pieces in half so each pieces measures 2½ x 6 inches (6.4 x 15.2 cm). Use the template and cut the edges in the same way as step 5. Position the cut linen on the sides of your other tree sections **(A)**.

7 Sew all the strips together. When sewing angled strips together, you need to offset the edges by about ¼ inch (6 mm). Sew the three complete strips together to create your tree.

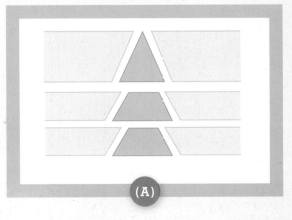

(A)

8 To create your tree trunk: Cut a piece of brown fabric that measures 2 x 2½ inches (5.1 x 6.4 cm). Cut another linen rectangle in half to create two 2 x 6-inch (5.1 x 15.2 cm) linen strips. Sew together these three pieces along the short edges, with the trunk fabric in the middle.

9 Sew your tree trunk strip to the bottom of your pieced tree.

10 Trim your pieced top to 8½ inches (21.6 cm) wide. Make a quilt sandwich with the top, batting, and backing, then pin or baste all layers in place. Quilt as desired.

11 Bind the edges of the mat, using the strip of binding fabric (pages 15–17).

the circle

1 Trace a circle onto the cardstock using a plate or other round object with a diameter of approximately 7½ inches (19 cm). Cut out your template.

2 Sew the fabric strips together along the 10-inch (25.4 cm) side, using a ¼-inch (6 mm) seam allowance throughout. Your pieced square will measure approximately 10 x 10½ inches (25.4 x 26.7 cm).

3 Lay your circle template on your pieced square. Cut around your template, leaving approximately ¼ inch (6 mm) extra around the edge of the circle template (B).

4 Lay your pieced circle, right side down, on a square of aluminum foil that measures approximately 12 inches square (30.5 cm). Lay your cardstock template on top of the pieced circle.

5 Using your fingers, fold the foil over and around the edges of the circle template. Move your fingers around the circle slowly, pressing carefully and smoothing out the edge as much as possible.

6 Press the edges with a hot, dry iron. Move around the edge of the circle slowly, pressing down the fabric well along the edge of the circle. Once finished, the tin foil will be hot. Let cool before unwrapping the foil.

7 Unwrap the foil carefully. The fabric should be pressed well around the entire circle template. Remove the cardboard template from inside your fabric piece.

8 Center your circle, right side up, on top of the square of background fabric. Pin in place.

9 Make a quilt sandwich with the pinned circle/background fabric, batting, and backing fabric, as you would a quilt top, then pin or baste all layers in place. Topstitch around the edge of your circle, stitching through all layers of your quilt sandwich and securing the layers in place.

10 Quilt as desired and bind your mat (pages 15–17).

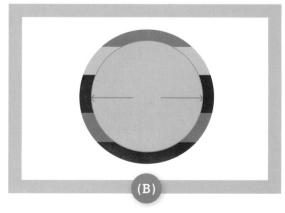

(B)

Rudolph Hoop Ornament

Small, adorable, and quick, this ornament is blissfully easy to sew. Make a bunch as teacher gifts or for your co-workers… just be sure to make one for yourself, too.

handmade by **ANGELA MITCHELL**

fabric & such

Brown fabric scraps for reindeer

1 piece of background fabric, 6 inches square (15.2 cm)

1 piece of print fabric (for backing), 6 inches square (15.2 cm)

1 piece of fusible web, 7 inches square (17.8 cm)

Embroidery hoop, 4 inches (10.2 cm) in diameter

Embroidery floss

Ribbon for hanging (optional)

tools

Templates (page 119)

finished size

4 inches (10.2 cm) in diameter

get started

1 Enlarge and cut out the templates.

2 Trace the shapes onto the fusible web square. Cut out the shapes roughly, then adhere them to the back of your fabric scraps, and then cut out the fabric shapes.

3 To make the reindeer face:

- Lay the background fabric on an ironing board. Unscrew the embroidery hoop and center the outer hoop on top of the fabric as a guideline.

- Pull the paper backing off the reindeer head piece and the two antler pieces, and center them in the middle of the hoop. When you are happy with their position, remove the hoop and press the pieces in place.

- Remove the backing paper from the remaining pieces and position and press them to the background fabric in the same way.

- Topstitch, using a short stitch length, ⅛ inch (3 mm) from the edge and around all pieces. If you like, use a contrasting thread to make a dark outline.

- Embroider the reindeer features as desired, using an embroidery needle and floss.

4 To assemble the ornament:

- Layer first the inner hoop, backing fabric (right side facing down), and then the finished reindeer appliqué (right side facing up). Center the outer hoop on top. Make sure the screw is loosened (and at the top center). Carefully press the outer hoop down onto the inner hoop.

- Trim the excess background and backing fabric as close to hoop as possible. Tie a ribbon on the screw and hang, if desired.

gift card giver

Rather than just sticking gift cards in a store-bought envelope, why not customize them with a handmade holder? This project doubles as a tree ornament.

handmade by MO BEDELL

fabric & such *(to make one)*

Assorted fabric scraps

1 square of batting, 4½ x 5½ inches (11.4 x 14 cm)

Embroidery floss

Assorted small buttons for decorating the tree appliqué

Binding scrap (optional)

1 piece of ribbon or metallic floss, 6 inches (15.2 cm) long

tools

Basic Patchwork Kit (page 9)

Templates (page 119)

Double-sided tape (optional)

finished size

4 x 4¾ inches (10 x 12 cm)

seam allowance

¼ inch (6 mm)

get started

1 Enlarge the templates and cut them out. Cut out a set of pattern pieces from the fabric scraps.

> Tip: *If using silk, stick the pattern piece directly to the fabric with double-sided tape. This will make it easier to precisely cut out the small, slippery pieces.*

2 Sew the tree pieces together to make the front of the ornament, as follows. As a general rule, press seams open as you sew; if using silk, press the seams toward the darker color.

- With right sides facing, stitch the A pieces onto both sides of the B (trunk) piece. Press and set aside.

- With right sides facing, stitch the C piece to the left side of D (the tree triangle). The top where the two pieces are joined will have a little overlap, so square off the piece using a rotary cutter and ruler. This gives you a clean edge to line up with piece E.

- With right sides facing, stitch E to the right side of D. Press and square up the edges.

- With right sides facing, pin the bottom edge of the C-D-E pieced section to the top of the A-B-A pieced section. Stitch and press.

3 Pin the finished front piece to the square of batting. Quilt around the tree shape by hand with embroidery floss, or by machine.

4 When you have finished quilting, make sure your piece is nicely pressed. Square up the edges using a rotary cutter. The finished measurements should be 4¼ x 5¼ inches (10.8 x 13.3 cm).

5 Decorate your tree! Lay out the buttons to see how many and where you want them to be. Use a disappearing fabric marker to mark a placement dot under each button before hand sewing it in place. The front is now finished.

6 The back pieces F and G will be used to make an envelope-style closure with the top section overlapping the bottom, so you can slide a gift card or other small gift inside. You have two options for finishing the overlapped edges: either make a ¼-inch (6 mm) double-fold hem or attach premade binding (pages 15–17).

7 If using ribbon to hang the ornament, fold the 6-inch (15.2 cm) piece of ribbon in half to make a loop. Pin it to the front (right) side the ornament, with the ends at the top center point of the tree, slightly overlapping the raw edge. If using embroidery floss, skip this step and add the hanging loop later (in step 10).

8 To assemble the ornament:

- Lay the hemmed F piece (top back) on top of the front piece with right sides together and aligning top and side raw edges (A). Pin carefully, leaving the pinned ribbon in place.

- Pin the G piece (bottom back) on top, right side facing down, aligning the bottom and side raw edges.

- Stitch around all four sides of the ornament.

9 Carefully clip each corner and turn the ornament right side out. Gently push out each corner with a turning tool.

variations

Just about any fabric will work for these ornaments, so your possibilities for personalizing them are endless. Use your imagination!

- Try a cashmere and tweed version.

- Embroider a blanket stitch around the edges (page 13).

- Use the foundation piecing method to stitch kimono scraps together, then cut the tree and stump out of the patchworked piece.

10 If using embroidery floss to hang the ornament, thread a length of metallic floss through an embroidery needle. Starting on the inside of the ornament, push the needle out the center top and the back through, being careful to leave a generous loop of embroidery floss on the outside. Tie the ends together on the inside of the ornament.

11 Now insert your gift and hang the ornament on the tree! (You could also hide a sweet little note inside.)

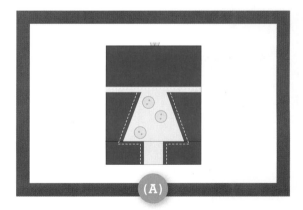

(A)

drawstring wine bag

Need the perfect hostess gift for a last-minute holiday party? I thought so! These drawstring bags put a refreshingly modern spin on an old classic.

handmade by **CHRISTINA LANE**

fabric & such

¼ yard (.2 m) of linen (exterior fabric)

¼ yard (.2 m) of lining fabric

Assorted pieces of fabric (for medallions), at least 5 inches square (12.7 cm), including a solid white scrap

Cardstock

1¼ yards (1.1 m) of ribbon (for drawstring), ⅜ inch (9.5 mm) wide

tools

Basic Patchwork Kit (page 9)

Templates (page 123)

Craft knife

Empty wine bottle (optional)

Safety pin

finished size

11 ¾ x 6 inches (30 x 15.2 cm) when flat

seam allowance

¼ inch (6 mm) unless otherwise indicated

get started

1 Copy the medallion and bag bottom circle temples onto the cardstock. Use the craft knife to carefully cut along the lines of the medallion circles. Cut out the bag bottom template piece.

2 Cut out the following pieces from the fabrics.

From the linen (exterior fabric):

- 2 rectangles, measuring 12 x 6½ inches (30.5 x 16.5 cm).

- 1 bag bottom, using the template.

- 1 square measuring 5 inches (12.7 cm).

From the lining fabric:

- 2 rectangles, each measuring 11¾ x 6½ inches (30 x 16.5 cm).

- 1 bag bottom, using the template.

From the scraps (use the white scrap and three different fabric colors, referred to as fabrics A, B, and C per the medallion template):

- 1 square measuring 3 inches (7.6 cm) from white fabric.

- 1 square measuring 3 inches (7.6 cm) from fabric A.

- 2 squares, each measuring 4 inches (10.2 cm) from fabric B.

- 2 squares, each measuring 5 inches (12.7 cm) from fabric C.

3 Cut the ribbon in half to make two 22-inch (55.9 cm) lengths.

4 To make the center of the medallion, use a disappearing fabric marker to trace the desired medallion appliqué shape onto the right side of the white fabric square. This example shows the tree shape.

- Pin the white, traced fabric on top of fabric A, both with right sides up.

- Stitch around the traced image, using a short stitch length. When you reach the beginning of the stitching, pull the piece away from the machine and clip the threads so they remain long. Pull the threads from the front of the piece to the back and knot them together before clipping the threads. This will ensure that the stitching does not unravel.

- Use a sharp pair of scissors to cut away the fabric on the inside of the stitching, leaving a scant seam allowance next to the stitching (A).

5 To make the first round "window" that reveals the center appliqué:

- Pin the two fabric B squares together with right sides facing.

- Center the circle A template on one of the wrong sides and trace around the circle.

- Stitch around the traced circle, backstitching to secure.

- Cut out the circle inside the stitches, leaving a ¼-inch (6 mm) seam allowance. Clip into the seam allowance, almost to the stitching, every ½-inch (1.3 cm) around the inside of the circle.

- Push the top fabric through the circle to the back side, so the right side of the fabric is showing on both sides of the piece (B). Press well.

- Designate a back side and clip the back fabic piece to ⅜-inch (9.5 mm) around the circle.

6 To make the second "window," follow the instructions in step 5, using the two fabric C squares and tracing around circle template B.

7 To make the window in the wine bag:

- Center and trace the circle template C on the wrong side of the 5-inch square (12.7 cm) cut from exterior fabric.

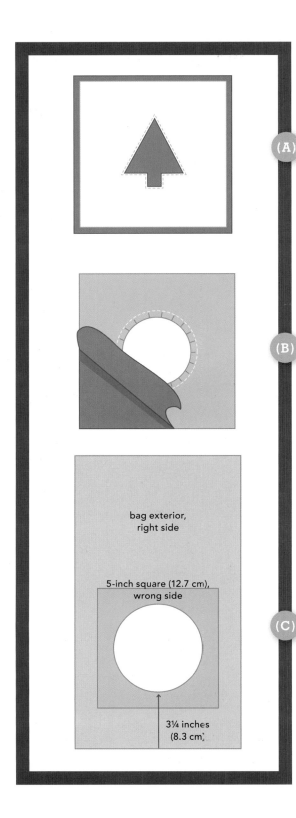

(A)

(B)

bag exterior,
right side

5-inch square (12.7 cm),
wrong side

3¼ inches
(8.3 cm)

(C)

- Pin this square onto one of the exterior pieces, right sides together. Make sure the bottom of the traced circle (not the bottom of the linen square) is centered and positioned 3¼ inches (8.3 cm) from the bottom of the exterior linen piece (C).

- Stitch on the traced line, cut and trim the seam allowance as in step 5, and turn the square to the inside of the bag. Press.

8 To assemble the appliqués:

- Pin fabric circle B over the medallion center, centering the appliqué in the opening.

- Stitch the appliqué in place by hand or machine with a ⅛ to ¼ inch (3 to 6 mm) seam allowance. If stitching by machine, clip the thread long enough to pull to the back and tie off.

- Center the fabric circle C on top of the first layers and stitch in the same way.

- Center the stitched medallion behind the window in the bag exterior and stitch once again (D).

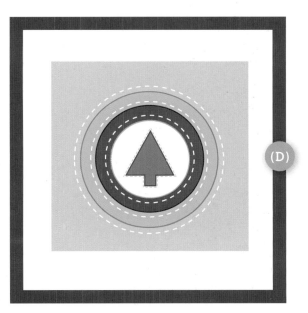

(D)

9 To make the exterior with a drawstring casing, do the following. (If you prefer a handle instead of a drawstring, see the Handle Variation box.)

- On the wrong side of one exterior piece, make a mark 1¾ inches (4.4 cm) from the top on both sides, then make another mark ½ inch (1.3 cm) from the first (E).

- With right sides together, stitch the exterior bag pieces together with a ½-inch (1.3 cm) seam allowance, but do not sew between the marks made on the pieces. Backstitch to lock the beginning and end of the stitches.

- With right sides together, pin the bag bottom to the bag body. Stitch in place. Turn right side out and press the seam.

Tip: *Insert a wine bottle into the bag to help press the seam.*

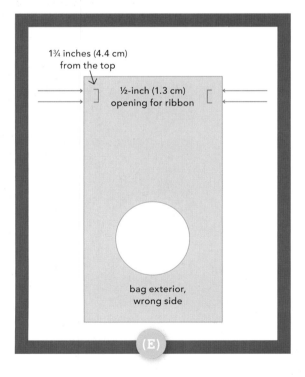

1¾ inches (4.4 cm) from the top

½-inch (1.3 cm) opening for ribbon

bag exterior, wrong side

(E)

variation

Customize the center medallion to make a gift bag that's perfect for a birthday, another holiday, or monogrammed for the recipient.

10 To make the lining:

- Pin the front and back lining pieces with right sides together.

- Stitch the sides, leaving a 4-inch (10.2 cm) opening in the middle of one side. Press seams open.

- With right sides together, pin the lining bottom to the lining body and stitch. Leave the lining wrong side out.

11 To assemble the bag:

- Slide the exterior piece inside the lining, right sides facing. Pin the two pieces together along the top.

- Stitch all the way around the top, then turn right side out through the hole in the lining.

- Stitch the opening in the lining closed, either by hand with an invisible stitch, or by machine, stitching close to the edge of the fabric.

■ Push the lining to the inside of the bag. The top of the lining should sit ¼ inch (6 mm) below the top of the bag. Press the top of the bag to hold the lining in place, and then topstitch around the top of the bag, just below where the lining meets the exterior piece.

■ To complete the drawstring casing, use a disappearing fabric marker to draw a line just above and below the openings in the side seam, across the width of the bag on both sides. Stitch along both lines all the way around the bag.

12 To add the drawstrings:

■ Attach a safety pin onto the end of one length of the ribbon. Push the safety pin into the casing through one of the side openings and thread it around the entire bag until the safety pin reaches the same hole. Push through the opening and draw the ribbon evenly through the bag.

■ Repeat with the second length of ribbon, starting at the opening on the opposite side.

■ Press the entire bag and insert your bottle of choice!

handle variation

If you prefer a handle rather than a drawstring, here's what you do:

■ Cut two rectangles measuring 10 x 2 inches (25.4 x 5.1 cm) for the handle. For the sample shown, one was cut from exterior fabric and one from a print.

■ Follow the instructions for steps 1 through 8, but skip the first part of step 9 (marking the drawstring casing). Simply stitch the front and back exterior pieces together along the sides, right sides facing, with a ½-inch (1.3 cm) seam allowance. Press seams open.

■ With right sides together, pin the bag bottom to the bag body. Stitch in place. Turn right side out and press the seam.

■ To make the handle, stitch the two handle pieces together along each long side. Turn the piece right side out and press. Edge stitch along each side of the handle.

■ Pin the handle to the exterior piece on the right side, centering the handle on the side seams and matching the raw edges of the handle and bag. Stitch together with slightly less than a ¼-inch (6 mm) seam allowance, backstitching over the piece a few times. A wine bottle is heavy, so this needs to be secure!

■ Continue following the instructions to make the wine bag. When inserting the exterior into the lining (step 11), make sure the handles are tucked between the exterior and the lining.

christmas in the city quilt

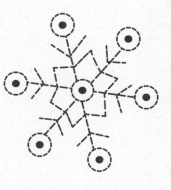

This quilt, with its modern take on traditional holiday colors, is an homage to Christmastime in the big city, perfect for cozying up a downtown loft.

handmade by JOHN Q. ADAMS

---

fabric & such

1¼ yards (1.1 m) of light purple fabric

1⅓ yards (1.2 m) of dark purple fabric

¼ yard (.2 m) each of five or more coordinating prints

4½ yards (4.1 m) of backing fabric

Double-sized batting

⅔ yard (.6 m) of binding fabric

tools

Basic Patchwork Kit (page 9)

finished size

60 x 77 inches (152.4 x 195.6 cm)

seam allowance

¼ inch (6 mm) unless otherwise indicated

get started

1 Cut the following pieces from the fabrics.

From light purple:

- 2 strips, each measuring 7½ inches (19 cm) x the width of the fabric.

- 5 strips, each measuring 3½ inches (8.9 cm) x the width of the fabric.

- 1 strip measuring 4½ inches (11.4 cm) x the width of the fabric.

From dark purple:

- 7 strips measuring 3½ inches (8.9 cm) x the width of the fabric.

- 1 strip measuring 7½ inches (19 cm) x the width of the fabric.

- 3 strips, each measuring 4½ inches (11.4 cm) x the width of the fabric.

From the assorted prints:

- 11 strips, each measuring 3½ inches (8.9 cm) x the width of the fabric.

- 6 strips, each measuring 4½ inches (11.4 cm) x the width of the fabric.

From binding fabric: 7 strips, each measuring 2½ inches (6.4 cm) x the width of the fabric.

2 Group the strips into the following combinations and stitch them together **(A)** to create 12 pieced strips measuring 10½ x 44 inches (26.7 x 111.8 cm) each. Press seams open.

quantity	left 3½-inch-wide (8.9 cm) strip	middle 4½-inch-wide (11.4 cm) strip	right 3½-inch-wide (8.9 cm) strip
3	Purple	Print	Dark purple
3	Print	Dark purple	Print
2	Light purple	Print	Light purple
1	Print	Light purple	Print
1	Dark purple	Print	Light purple

quantity	left 7½-inch-wide (19 cm) strip	right 3½-inch-wide (8.9 cm) strip
2	Light purple	Print
1	Dark purple	Print

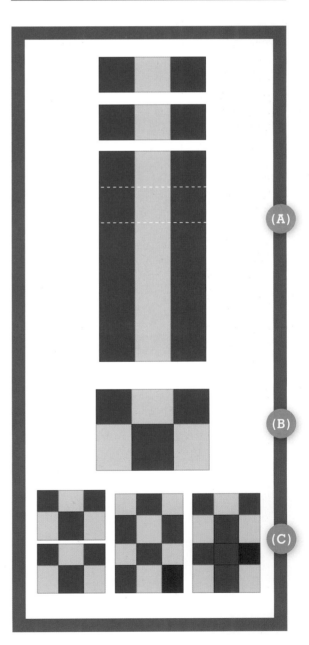

(A)

(B)

(C)

3 Cut the following from each pieced strip:

- 5 rectangles, each measuring 3½ x 10½ inches (8.9 x 26.7 cm).

- 5 rectangles, each measuring 4½ x 10½ inches (11.4 x 26.7 cm).

4 Create a series of blocks by stitching the 3½ x 10½-inch (8.9 x 26.7 cm) pieced rectangles to the top of the 4½ x 10½-inch (11.4 x 26.7 cm) rectangles (**B**). Be sure to alternate prints and solids in some of the blocks, and let the solids touch to form continuous fields of color in others. Each quilt block will measure 7½ x 10½ inches (19 x 26.7 cm). Make a total of 66 blocks.

> **Tip:** *Chain-piecing (page 11) is an effective technique to use here!*

5 Lay out the quilt top in rows of six blocks across by 11 blocks down. Start at the top with blocks containing primarily dark purples, and gradually introduce the light purple solids as you make your way down the quilt. If you get stuck with blocks that you don't think work well in a particular spot, just use your scraps to quickly whip up another block that will fit your layout scheme better (**C**).

6 Piece the blocks together in rows of 6, and then join the rows together.

7 Make a quilt sandwich with the quilt top, batting, and backing. Baste all layers together and quilt them by machine or hand. Trim any excess batting and backing fabric.

8 Stitch the binding strips together end-to-end to make one long strip and bind the quilt (pages 15-17).

woven stocking

Shop from your fabric stash to make coordinated stockings for the whole family using this neat "woven" patchwork piecing technique.

handmade by **AMANDA CARESTIO**

fabric & such
1 piece of linen, 15 x 18 inches
    (38.1 x 45.7 cm)
1 fat quarter (45.7 x 55.9 cm), plus assorted
    print fabric scraps
½ yard (.5 m) of backing fabric
1 piece of batting, 15 x 18 inches
    (38.1 x 45.7 cm)
Button, 1⅛ inches (2.9 cm) in diameter

tools
Basic Patchwork Kit (page 9)
Template (page 119)

finished size
8 x 16 inches (20.3 x 40.6 cm)

seam allowance
¼ inch (6 mm) unless otherwise indicated

get started

1 Cut multiple strips from the scrap fabrics to 1½ inches (3.8 cm) wide. Stitch them together end-to-end to make one long strip about 95 to 100 inches (241.3 to 254 cm) long. For a scrappier look, cut any long pieces apart and stitch them back together elsewhere in the strip.

2 Enlarge the template and cut it out. Use it to cut one stocking shape from the linen, adding about 2 inches (5.1 cm) extra around the edges.

3 Cut a vertical line through the stocking shape 1¼ inches (3.2 cm) from the right edge (A). Measure the length of the stocking from top to bottom and cut a section that ong from the pieced strip. Stitch it between the two pieces you just separated. Press.

4 Cut a horizontal line through the stocking about 2 to 3 inches (5.1 to 7.6 cm) down from the top edge, cutting through the pieced strip you just added (B). Measure across the width and cut a section from the pieced strip. Stitch it between the two pieces you just separated. Press.

5 Continue working in this way, alternating between vertical and horizontal cuts, through the rest of the stocking front. In the sample shown, vertical strips are placed 1¼ inches (3.2 cm) apart and the horizontal strips are 2½ inches (6.4 cm) apart. Make your last pieced strip section very scrappy so it blends well with the rest of the grid.

6 Lay the stocking front on top of the piece of batting, right side up. Place the fat quarter face down on top of the stocking front, lining up the top straight edge. Stitch the layers together along the top edge, then fold the backing to the back, leaving a bit showing on the top edge (C). Cut the batting and fat quarter backing to match the shape of the stocking front.

7 Quilt the layers together as desired. The sample shows several rows of straight stitches sewn through each of the pieced strips.

8 Line up the top of the template and the top finished edge of the stocking, and cut the stocking to size.

9 To make the binding, cut several 3-inch-wide (7.6 cm) strips from the scrap fabric. You'll need about 48 inches (121.9 cm). Fold and press the strip in half and attach as double-fold binding (pages 15–17).

10 To make the hanging loop, cut a 3 x 10–inch (7.6 x 25.4 cm) scrap of fabric. Fold under the short ends, and fold the strip in half so the long edges meet with right sides together. Stitch along the long edge, and turn the strip right side out. Press flat with the seam in the back, and stitch down the center of the strip.

11 Fold the strip in half and sandwich the stocking corner between the ends of the strip. Stitch the ends in place, stitching through all the layers. Add the button on top of the stitching for decoration.

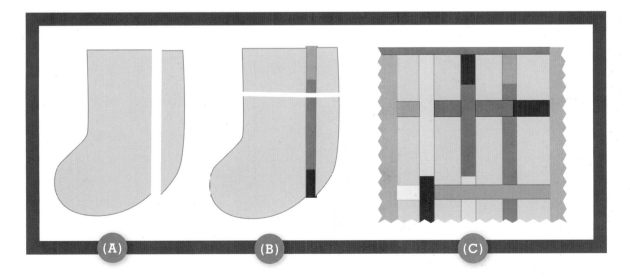

(A)   (B)   (C)

holiday shopping list folio

The holidays are no time to be disorganized. Whip up this indispensable organizer in your most favorite holiday fabrics so you can stay organized and calm, even when frazzled by the shopping hordes.

handmade by TERRI HARLAN

fabric & such

Assorted pieces of fabric, at least 2 inches square (5.1 cm)

1 fat quarter (45.7 x 55.9 cm) of linen blend fabric

1 fat quarter (45.7 x 55.9 cm) of cotton fabric (for interior)

1 piece of heavyweight fusible interfacing, 8 x 11 inches (20.3 x 27.9 cm)

Embroidery floss

Elastic band

1 piece of fusible fleece, 8 x 11 inches (20.3 x 27.9 cm)

Button, 1 inch (2.5 cm) in diameter

Notebook, 4 x 7 inches (10.2 x 17.8 cm)

Pen

tools

Basic Patchwork Kit (page 9)

finished size

5 x 7 inches (12.7 x 17.8 cm) when closed

seam allowance

¼ inch (6 mm) unless otherwise indicated

get started

1 Cut out the following pieces from the fabrics.

From fabric scraps: 21 squares, each measuring 2 inches (5.1 cm).

From linen blend fabric:

- 1 piece measuring 9 x 11 inches (22.9 x 27.9 cm).

- 1 piece measuring 3½ x 11 inches (8.9 x 27.9 cm).

From cotton fabric:

- 1 piece measuring 8 x 11 inches (20.3 x 27.9 cm).

- 1 square measuring 5 inches (12.7 cm).

2 Prepare the interior pieces:

- Fuse the heavyweight interfacing to the same size cotton piece, following the manufacturer's instructions. Set aside.

- Fold the remaining cotton piece in half diagonally to form a triangle. This will become the angled pocket on the left side. Set aside.

- Fold the larger linen piece in half to make a 4½ x 11-inch (11.4 x 27.9 cm) piece for the inside pocket. Stitch along the folded edge ¼ inch (6 mm) from the top. Use a disappearing fabric marker to write a message in the bottom right-hand corner, allowing about ¾ inches (1.9 cm) on the bottom and right edges for the seams. Embroider as desired using an embroidery needle and floss.

3 Put together the interior:

- Lay the fused interior piece on a flat surface. Pin the embroidered pocket on top, aligning raw edges on the bottom and sides.

- Fold the interior in half, or measure to find the center point. Use the fabric marker to draw a line ½ inch (1.3 cm) away from the center on both sides (A). Stitch along the drawn lines to form a pen slot, backstitching at the top for extra strength.

- Pin the angled pocket set aside in step 2 in the lower left-hand corner, on top of the linen pocket, aligning raw edges. Baste in place.

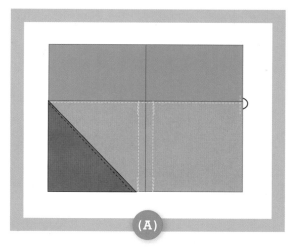

(A)

- Find the center of the right-hand edge and pin the elastic band at that point. Stitch over the band a few times to secure it, making sure not to stitch over the glued section of the band (this will break your needle).

4 Make the exterior:

- Lay out the 2-inch (5.1 cm) assorted squares in an order that you like, with three rows of

seven squares. Stitch the squares together in rows, then stitch the rows together. Press.

- With right sides together, pin the remaining linen piece to the top edge of the patchwork, matching up the 11-inch (27.9 cm) edges. Stitch and press open. You should now have a large piece measuring 8 x 11 inches (20.3 x 27.9 cm). Square up this piece if needed.

- For a more finished look, topstitch along the linen about ¼ inch (6 mm) from the patchwork.

- Fuse the fleece interfacing to the wrong side of the patchwork, following the manufacturer's instructions. This will make the cover soft and cushioned as well as give it a little structure.

- Match up the exterior and interior to check for the placement of the button. Mark on the exterior piece where the elastic is, and hand sew the button about 1 inch (2.5 cm) from the raw edge at that location.

5 Assemble the list taker:

- Pin the interior and exterior together with right sides facing, the corners aligned, and the elastic tucked between the layers.

- Stitch together on all sides, leaving a 5-inch (12.7 cm) opening on the top edge for turning.

- Turn the pieces right side out through the opening. Use a turning tool to gently push out the corners.

- Press the list taker flat, neatly folding in the seam allowance at the opening.

- Topstitch a ⅛-inch (3 mm) seam around the entire perimeter to close the edges.

6 Insert the 4 x 6 (10.2 x 17.8 cm) notebook and your favorite pen to complete the package.

Patchwork Spiral Ornaments

Scrap sewers: this is the perfect project for you! Use even the tiniest bits of your favorite prints to whip up these adorable ornaments, perfect for your tree or to top off a wrapped gift.

handmade by **MARILYN BUTLER**

fabric & such

2 strips of fabric (A), each 1 x 18 inches (2.5 x 45.7 cm)

2 strips of fabric (B), each 1 x 18 inches (2.5 x 45.7 cm)

1 piece of ribbon, ¼ to ½ inch (6 mm to 2.5 cm) wide x 10 inches (25.4 cm) long

Polyester fiberfill

finished size

3½ inches square (8.9 cm), not including hanging loop

seam allowance

¼ inch (6 mm); press seams open to reduce bulk.

get started

1 For each side of the ornament, cut the following pieces from the fabrics A or B as indicated. Line them up in order, or write the number in a corner seam allowance to keep track.

#1	A	1 inch square (2.5 cm)
#2	B	1 inch square (2.5 cm)
#3	B	1 x 1½ inches (2.5 x 3.8 cm)
#4	A	1 x 1½ inches (2.5 x 3.8 cm)
#5	A	1 x 2 inches (2.5 x 5.1 cm)
#6	B	1 x 2 inches (2.5 x 5.1 cm)
#7	A	1 x 2½ inches (2.5 x 6.4 cm)
#8	B	1 x 2½ inches (2.5 x 6.4 cm)
#9	B	1 x 3 inches (2.5 x 7.6 cm)
#10	A	1 x 3 inches (2.5 x 7.6 cm)
#11	B	1 x 3½ inches (2.5 x 8.9 cm)
#12	A	1 x 3½ inches (2.5 x 8.9 cm)
#13	A	1 x 4 inches (2.5 x 10.2 cm)

2 Stitch the pieces together one at a time in numbered order, according to the diagram (**A**). Repeat for the other side of the ornament.

3 Bring the ends of the ribbon together to form a loop. Lay the loop on the right side of one block, with the raw ends extending about ½ to ¾ inch

(1.3 to 1.9 cm) beyond one corner (**B**). Pin the other block, right side down, on top of the first block, catching the ribbon in place.

4 Stitch together the outer edges of the ornament, catching the ribbon in the seam and leaving a 2-inch (5.1 cm) opening on one side. Clip the corners and turn the ornament right side out through the opening. Use a turning tool to gently push out the corners.

5 Lightly but evenly, stuff the ornament with the polyester fiberfill. Hand sew the opening closed.

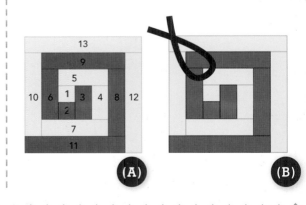

greetings from antarctica! quilted pillows

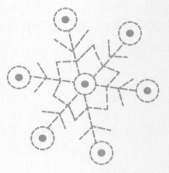

If your holidays aren't complete without a touch of whimsy, consider making some of these adorable foundation-pieced pillows.

handmade by SONJA CALLAGHAN

fabric & such

POLAR BEAR BLOCK, FABRIC, AND NOTIONS

1 fat quarter (45.7 x 55.9 cm) of aqua fabric (for background)

¼ yard (.23 m) each of black fabric and fabric color of choice (for scarf)

½ yard (.5 m) of white fabric

2 black buttons (for large eyes)

2 black buttons (for small eyes)

PENGUIN BLOCK, FABRIC, AND NOTIONS

½ yard (.5 m) of aqua fabric (for background)

1 fat quarter (45.7 x 55.9 cm) each of orange, black, and white fabric

1 fat quarter (45.7 x 55.9 cm) of red fabric, if making hat

LARGE PENGUIN NOTIONS

2 black buttons (for eyes)

1 white button (for hat pom-pom, if making)

SMALL PENGUIN NOTIONS

2 white buttons with four holes (for eyes)

2 black buttons for pupils

1 white button (for hat pom-pom, if making), ¾ inch (1.9 cm) in diameter

FOR BOTH PILLOWS

1¾ yards (1.6 m) of white fabric

½ yard (.5 m) of gray fabric

¼ yard (.23 m) of aqua fabric (for back of pillow)

1 fat quarter (45.7 x 55.9 cm) of coordinating fabric (for back of pillow), or 1 yard (.9 m) if using a directional print

1 piece of low loft batting, 22 inches square (55.9 cm)

Embroidery floss in white and black

White plastic non-separating zipper, 16 inches (40.6 cm) long

Pillow insert, 18 inches square (45.7 cm)

tools

Basic Patchwork Kit (page 9)

Templates (pages 120–121)

Pinking shears or pinking blade on rotary cutter (optional)

Zipper foot

finished size

18 inches square (45.7 cm)

seam allowance

¼ inch (6 mm) unless otherwise indicated

get started

1 Cut out the following pieces from the fabrics. From white fabric:

- 2 strips, each measuring 1½ inches (3.8 cm) x the width of the fabric, for front sashing.

- 1 square measuring 22 inches (55.9 cm), for backing behind the front block.

- 1 piece measuring 6½ x 19 inches (16.5 x 48.3 cm), for backing behind the back block.

- 2 pieces, each measuring 1½ x 2 inches (3.8 x 5.1 cm), for ends of the zipper.

- 2 strips, each measuring 3½ inches (8.9 cm) x the width of the fabric, for binding.

From gray fabric:

- 2 strips, each measuring 3½ inches (8.9 cm) x the width of the fabric, for front sashing.

- 1 strip measuring 3 x 19 inches (7.6 x 48.3 cm), for the zipper flap.

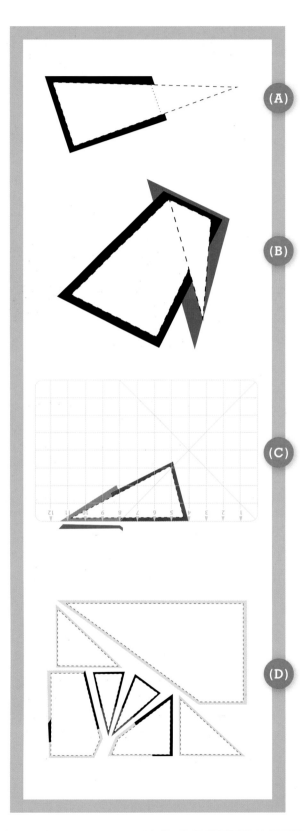

From the aqua fabric (for back of pillow):

- 1 strip measuring 11 x 6½ inches (27.9 x 16.5 cm).

- 1 strip measuring 2½ x 6½ inches (6.4 x 16.5 cm).

From coordinating fabric: 1 piece measuring 13 x 19 inches (33 x 48.3 cm).

2 Enlarge and cut out the templates of choice. Stitch one large center block for the front and one mini block for the back, as follows:

- Place your first piece underneath its spot on the pattern template, right side facing away from the pattern, and pin it in place. Make sure the seam allowance extends past the sewing lines on the pattern by holding it up the light so you can see the fabric through the paper.

- Carefully slide the pattern face up (with the fabric pinned underneath) under your presser foot and stitch in place along the indicated line (A).

- Line up the raw edges of your first and second piece, with right sides facing (B). Carefully slide your pattern face up under your presser foot and sew the line between the two pieces.

- Sew up each section using this process. Trim all the seam allowances to a nice ¼ inch (6 mm) (C), and pin to secure the corners of the larger pieces.

- When all the sections are done, sew them together in alphabetical order (D). When aligning the sections, place their right sides together watching closely that you line up the paper edges of each pattern.

- Repeat this process for the mini block on the back.

> *Do not sew on the buttons yet; that will be done after quilting.*

3 Trim the front block to 12½ inches square (31.8 cm) and the back block to 6½ inches square (16.5 cm). Set aside the back block.

4 To create the eyes for the large penguin (if making), make white circle appliqués for each eye as follows:

- Cut three pieces measuring 3 inches square (7.6 cm) from the white fabric.

- Stack these three pieces one on top of the other, and on the top square trace the outer eye circle from the template, adding ¼ inch (6 mm) for seam allowance.

- Carefully stitch around the circle, through all three layers. Trim the seam allowance to ⅛ inch (3 mm) using pinking shears, or snip around the edge of the seam allowance.

- Pull one layer away from the other two, pinch it lengthwise, and cut a slit down the middle ¼ inch (6 mm) from the stitching line at each end.

- Turn the circle inside out through the slit. Use a turning tool to gently push out the seam so that the eye circle is smooth. Press.

- Repeat to make a second eye.

- Pin the two circles in place on the penguin face, slit side down, and hand sew with a blind stitch to the pillow top.

5 To assemble the front of the pillow:

- Stitch a strip of white sashing to both sides of the block, trimming the length to fit. Press the seams.

- Attach the remaining white sashing to the top and bottom of the block, again trimming the length to fit. Press the seams.

- In the same way, stitch gray sashing around the white sashing, first on the sides, then on the top and bottom. Press. The outer dimensions of the block should be 20½ inches square (50.8 cm).

6 To quilt the front:

- Make a quilt sandwich with the pillow front, batting, and white backing fabric.

- Before you baste together the layers, take a close look at all the white areas and trim back any uneven areas of colored seam allowances that show through. Check closely for a spot of orange at the beak tip of the penguin, if making. Remove any stray threads.

- Baste and quilt as desired. In the sample shown, the quilting outlines all the elements of the penguin and polar bear.

- Embroider a few snowflakes on the background using an embroidery needle and white floss, if desired.

- Trim and square up the quilted pillow front to 19 inches (48.3 cm). Make sure the penguin or polar bear motif remains symmetrical, with a 3-inch (7.6 cm) wide gray border all around.

- Hand sew any buttons needed for the eyes and the hat pom-pom, if making.

7 To make the back block:

- Trim back any seam edges showing through to the front of the back block set aside in step 3.

- Decide whether you want the block in the upper right or upper left corner of the block, and stitch the long and short aqua background strips cut in step 1 accordingly on the left and right edges of the block. This piece should now measure 6½ x 19 inches (16.5 x 48.3 cm).

- To provide some protection for the raw seams, pin the corresponding piece of white backing fabric behind the pieced strip. Baste together with a ⅛-inch (3 mm) seam.

8 To add the zipper:

- Press the gray zipper flap in half lengthwise. Stitch it to the bottom edge of the pieced strip, with right sides together and lining up the raw edges. Don't press this seam open yet.

- To each end of the zipper, stitch the white fabric ends cut in step 1 with right sides together and fairly close to the metal stoppers on the zipper. Press. Trim the zipper strip evenly to 19 inches (48.3 cm) long.

- Pin the zipper face down on the long edge (right side) of the coordinating fabric piece. Stitch together, using a zipper foot. Zigzag the seam allowance to prevent fraying. Press the zipper away from the coordinating fabric and topstitch along the seam close to the edge.

- Lay the zippered piece face up on a flat surface. Pin the previously prepared mini block and zipper flap on top, lining up the raw edges with the unsewn zipper edge, right sides together **(E)**

- Stitch, using the zipper foot. Zigzag the seam allowance and press so the gray zipper flap lies over the zipper.

- With the zipper closed, trim the bottom edge of the coordinating backing fabric so the entire pillow back measures 19 inches square (48.3 cm).

- Hand sew any buttons needed for the eyes and the hat pom-pom, if making.

9 To assemble the final pillow:

- Unzip the zipper a few inches, and pin the pillow front onto the pillow back, wrong sides together. Baste in place.

- Stitch the two white binding strips together end-to-end to make one long strip. Bind the edges of the pillow to cover the seam, mitering the corners (pages 15–17).

- Insert the pillow form and enjoy!

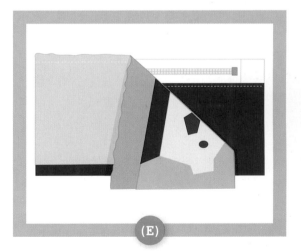

(E)

modern diamonds lap quilt

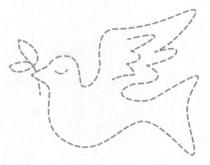

Built from diamond shapes that form an all-over diamond pattern, this quilt is both effortless and intricate, modern and traditional, complex yet deceptively simple in its construction.

handmade by **SCOTT HANSEN**

fabric & such

5 fat quarters (45.7 x 55.9 cm) each of assorted blue fabrics

5 fat quarters (45.7 x 55.9 cm) each of assorted green fabrics

8 fat quarters (45.7 x 55.9 cm) each of assorted white fabrics

7 fat quarters (45.7 x 55.9 cm) each of assorted red fabrics

7 fat quarters (45.7 x 55.9 cm) each of assorted black fabrics

3 yards (2.6 m) of backing fabric

1 yard (.9 m) of binding fabric (black print)

1 piece of batting, 65 x 70 inches (165.1 x 177.8 cm)

tools

Basic Patchwork Kit (page 9)

Template (page 121)

finished size

58½ x 62 inches (147.3 x 157.5 cm)

seam allowance

¼ inch (6 mm) unless otherwise indicated

get started

1 Enlarge and cut out the triangle template.

2 Cut out the following pieces from the fat quarters. First cut the number of strips listed from the short side of each fat quarter, then use the template to cut out triangles from the strip (A). The total number of triangles is listed for each color.

- Green: cut three 4-inch-wide (10.2 cm) strips and 16 triangles per fat quarter, for a total of 80 green triangles.

- Blue: cut three 4-inch-wide (10.2 cm) strips and 16 triangles per fat quarter, for a total of 80 blue triangles.

- White: from seven fat quarters, cut four 4-inch-wide (10.2 cm) strips and 20 triangles per fat quarter, for a total of 140 white triangles. Set aside the eighth white fat quarter to use later.

- Red: cut four 4-inch-wide (10.2 cm) strips and 23 triangles per fat quarter, for a total of 161 red triangles (you will use 160).

- Black: cut four 4-inch (10.2 cm) strips and 23 triangles per fat quarter, for a total of 161 black triangles (you will use 160).

3 Cut the border triangles:

- From the remaining white fat quarter, cut 20 rectangles, each measuring 2 ⅝ x 4½ inches (6.7 x 11.4 cm). Divide them into two stacks of 10.

- Cut one set of 10 rectangles in half diagonally (from corner to corner) as shown (B). Label these BTL (for border triangle left).

- Cut the remaining set of 10 rectangles in half diagonally in the other direction (from corner to corner) as shown (C). Label these BTR (for border triangle right).

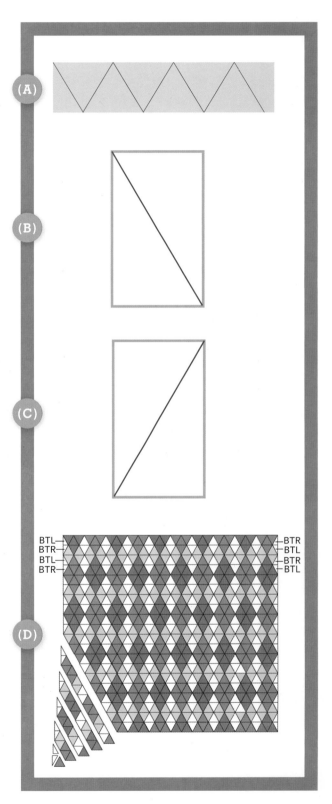

4 Lay out the triangles according to the color placement diagram **(D)**. Stitch the pieces together in rows diagonally.

5 When the quilt top is complete, make a quilt sandwich with the the quilt top, batting, and backing fabric, then pin or baste all layers in place. Quilt by machine or hand as desired. Trim any excess batting and backing fabric.

6 Stitch the binding strips together end-to-end to make one long strip and bind the quilt (pages 15–17).

sugar village tea towels

Enjoy playing around with buttons, rickrack, and other bits and bobs? Then you'll love making this sweet, perfectly giftable tea towel set.

handmade by JENNIFER DAVIS

fabric & such

Assorted fabric scraps for appliqué

Square tea towel or dinner napkin
  (the example is square)

Paper-backed fusible web

Small button for doorknob

4 medium to large mismatched buttons
  for towel corner accents

Rickrack, medium or jumbo size

tools

Basic Patchwork Kit (page 9)

Templates (page 120)

finished size

19½ x 19½ inches (49 x 49 cm)

get started

1 Enlarge and cut out the templates. Trace them onto the paper side of the fusible web. Cut out the fusible web, adding about ½ inch (1.3 cm) extra around each shape.

2 Fuse the cutout pieces onto the wrong side of the fabric scraps, then cut them out along the traced lines.

3 Using the project photograph for placement guidelines, begin fusing and edge stitching the pieces in place on the tea towel, starting with the main house shape. In the sample shown, each piece was outlined using coordinating thread and a short, narrow buttonhole stitch. Fuse and stitch the doors and windows on top of the house shape, ending with the roof.

4 Hand sew the small button in place as a doorknob.

5 Cut a circle measuring 2½ inches (6.4 cm) in diameter from a fabric scrap. Make a 1¼-inch

(3.2 cm) yo-yo. Center the yo-yo on the house above the door and hand sew in place.

6 Cut the rickrack trim into four pieces, each the length of one of your towel edges. Pin the pieces to the corresponding edges, with the raw ends abutting. Stitch down the center of the rickrack strips to secure, pivoting at the corners.

7 Hand sew the remaining buttons in place at the corners, covering up the raw ends of the rickrack.

gingerbread men embroidered apron

Bake up those goodies in style with a lovely linen apron framed in patchwork binding, decorated with cute bounding gingerbread men, and infused with holiday goodness. Modify the measurements to make some for your little helpers, too.

handmade by **CATHY GAUBERT**

fabric & such

1 yard (.9 m) of linen

¾ yard (.7 m) of seersucker (for back of waistband and ties)

7 coordinating red cotton prints, solid fat quarters, or pieces, for binding and waistband, each at least 2½ inches (6.4 cm) wide

1 piece of brown felt (for gingerbread men), 7 inches square (17.8 cm)

Fusible web

Embroidery floss or perle cotton in white, black, and red (for hand stitching details)

tools

Basic Patchwork Kit (page 9)

Templates (page 123)

finished size

35 x 18½ inches (88.9 x 46.9 cm)

seam allowance

¼ inch (6 mm) unless otherwise indicated

get started

1 Cut the linen to measure 36 x 17 inches (91.4 x 43.2 cm) for the apron body. Set aside. Cut the remaining linen to measure 18 x 10 inches (45.7 x 25.4 cm) for the apron pocket.

2 Copy and cut out the gingerbread men templates. Trace the gingerbread men onto the fusible web. Following manufacturer's instructions, iron the fusible web to the felt and cut out the gingerbread men. Refer to the project photograph for placement and iron the appliqués onto the apron pocket.

3 Appliqué the gingerbread men by machine stitching just inside their edges. Add details using an embroidery needle and three plies of white floss or perle cotton: Sew French knots for the buttons and straight stitches for the icing and mouths. Use a full, six-ply strand of black floss and make the eyes with French knots.

4 Transfer the phrase to the pocket using the template and hand stitch using red floss.

5 Cut the assorted coordinating fabrics into strips measuring 2½ inches (6.4 cm) wide; these will be used for the bindings and the apron waistband. Stack the strips and cut them into pieces measuring 5, 4, and 3 inches (12.7, 10.2, and 7.6 cm) long. Stitch the assorted pieces end-to-end to create a patchwork strip measuring 64 inches (162.6 cm) long; this piece will be the binding for the apron pocket. In the same way, stitch together a binding strip measuring 73 inches (185.4 cm) long; this will be the binding for the apron body.

6 Press seams open to decrease bulk. Fold and press to create two pieces of double-fold binding.

7 To bind the pocket, begin pinning the shorter binding strip at the upper right corner of the pocket, down the left edge (mitering the corners as you get to them), and ending at the bottom right corner. Stitch the binding in place using red thread and a zigzag stitch. Press.

8 Pin the pocket to the apron body by matching up the right raw edge of the pocket with the right edge of the apron body, leaving 4½ inches (11.4 cm) of apron body above and below the pocket. Beginning at the top right corner, stitch the pocket to the apron, stitching along the raw edge of the pocket, along the bottom edge, and up the left side of the pocket. Make additional stitches at the top left corner to add strength.

9 To bind the apron, begin pinning the remaining binding strip at the top right corner of the apron body, along the bottom edge, and ending at the top left corner. Be sure to miter the two corners as you get to them.

10 To make the patchwork waistband, gather up the remaining assorted ½-inch (6.4 cm) strips. Stitch assorted pieces end-to-end to create one patchwork strip measuring 36 inches (91.4 cm) long. Press the seams to one side. Set aside.

11 To make the ties, fold the seersucker fabric selvedge to selvedge. Cut two strips 5 inches wide (12.7 cm) and set aside. For each tie, fold under ¼-inch (6 mm) edge of the fabric all the way around and press. Fold over again and press. Be sure to miter the corners. Slightly increase your stitch length and topstitch around each tie, working ⅛ inch (3 mm) in from the edge. Topstitch again ¼ inch (6 mm) in from the previous stitched line. Set aside.

12 From the seersucker fabric, cut one strip measuring 36 x 2½ inches (91.4 x 6.4 cm). Pin the strip to the patchwork waistband, with right sides facing. Stitch along the length of one side only. Press the seam toward the patchwork side and fold right side out. Press again.

13 Turn the apron body so the back side is facing up and the raw edge is at the top. Pin the patchwork band, right side facing the apron, along the top edge. Stitch. Turn the apron so the front is now facing down, and press the seam toward the patchwork waistband. Now fold the waistband down.

14 To prepare the waistband for the insertion of the ties, fold in each side of the waistband so that the waistband side and the apron side are in line. Press.

15 Hand pleat the raw edge of one tie so that it measures about 1¼ inches (3.2 cm) wide. With the right side of the tie facing up, place about half of the pleated, raw edge onto the seersucker part of the waistband (this part of the waistband will have the wrong side facing). Hold in place and fold the patchwork part of the waistband down, sandwiching the tie between the front and back of the waistband. Pin through all layers. Do the same for the other tie. Next, fold and press the raw edge of the patchwork waistband under ¼ inch (6 mm). Slightly increase the stitch length and topstitch this edge to the apron. Reset the stitch length and then continue topstitching all the way around the waistband.

Polar Bear Dreams Ornament

This quick and cute project will give your home a wintry yet warm feeling. It's perfect for using up your most precious, tiny pieces of fabric!

handmade by **NICOLE VOS VAN AVEZATHE**

fabric & such

1 piece of white felt (for polar bear), 3 x 2 inches (7.6 x 5.1 cm)

1 piece of dark fabric, 3 x 6 inches (7.6 x 5.1 cm)

Assorted pieces of printed fabric, at least 1½ inches square (3.8 cm)

1 piece of batting, 7½ x 6½ inches (19 x 16.5 cm)

1 piece of felt (for backing), at least 5 inches square (12.7 cm)

Black embroidery floss

Wooden embroidery hoop, 5 inches (12.7 cm) in diameter

Coordinating ribbon (optional)

tools

Basic Patchwork Kit (page 9)

Templates (page 118)

Fabric glue

get started

1 Copy and cut out the polar bear templates. Cut out the shapes from the white felt.

2 From the assorted fabrics, cut fifteen 1½-inch squares (3.8 cm). Arrange them in three rows, each with five squares. Arrange the dark fabric, polar bear pieces, and assorted fabric squares as desired, using the project photograph as a guide. You may want to arrange darker fabric squares for contrast around the bear's head and paw. Keep in mind that some squares on the bottom row may not show when the pieced fabric is wrapped to the back.

3 Stitch the squares together in strips of five, then stitch the rows together. Stitch the dark fabric piece to the top edge of the top row.

4 Sandwich together the pieced block and batting, pinning the two layers in place, and quilt with a stitch-in-the-ditch approach along the vertical and horizontal seams.

5 Pin the felt pieces in place and stitch in place as close to the outer edge as possible. Using an embroidery needle and two strands of black embroidery floss, add the eyes, nose, ear accents, and claws to the bear, using the project photo as a guide.

6 Place the finished piece into the embroidery hoop and adjust it until you are happy with the position. The next step is to glue the fabric in place, before trimming away the bulk:

- With the fabric in place, unscrew the outer hoop to its widest point.

- Put tiny dots of fabric glue on the inside of the outer ring of the embroidery hoop. You want to add enough glue to make the ring stick to the fabric, but too much will soak into your piece.

- Replace the outer hoop while bending it wide, so the glue will not touch the fabric until the ring is in place.

- Tighten the ring and allow the glue to dry.

7 Use scissors to trim the edges of the fabric sandwich close to the back of the hoop.

8 Use the hoop as a template to cut the piece of backing felt to size, as large as the back of your hoop. Glue the circle of felt to the back of the hoop, and add a hanging loop to the top if desired, using a piece of coordinating ribbon and fabric glue.

boxed christmas stars quilt

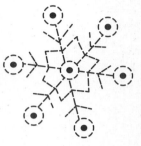

Is this quilt modern or is it traditional? Or both... and completely timeless besides! You'll be searching for every excuse to use this quilt year round.

handmade by DORREEN AGRES

fabric & such

1¼ yd (1.1 m) of assorted print for the stars

2 yards (1.8 m) of light or white fabric

4 yards (3.7 m) of red fabric (for background)

4 yards (3.7 m) of backing fabric

Lap size batting, about 70 x 70 inches (177.8 x 177.8 cm)

tools

Basic Patchwork Kit (page 9)

finished size

64 x 64 inches (162.6 x 162.6 cm)

seam allowance

¼ inch (6 mm) unless otherwise indicated

note

This quilt is made up of two block designs (see B). Block A, which forms the main body of the quilt, is a framed star. Block B, a corner block, is tucked around the edges to fill out the quilt. The corner without a white bar will be trimmed off.

get started

1 Cut out the following pieces for the blocks from the fabrics.

From print fabric:

- 40 squares, each measuring 3½ inches (8.9 cm), for the center of each block A.

- 160 squares, each measuring 2⅜ inches (6 cm), four to match each center square.

From the background fabric:

- 40 squares, each measuring 4¼ inches (10.8 cm), for block A.

- 160 squares, each measuring 2 inches (5.1 cm), for the corners of block A (four per block).

- 20 squares, each measuring 6½ inches (16.5 cm), for the centers of block B.

- 8 strips, each measuring 1½ inches (3.8 cm) x the width of the fabric.

- 50 strips, each measuring 1¼ x 8½ inches (3.2 x 21.6 cm) strips, for sashing.

- 7 strips, each measuring 2¼ inches (5.7 cm) x the width of the fabric, for binding.

From the white fabric:

- 8 strips, each measuring 3 inches (7.6 cm) x the width of the fabric.

- 8 strips, each measuring 4 inches (10.2 cm) x the width of the fabric.

- 40 strips, each measuring 3 x 1½ inches (3.8 cm), for the corners of block B.

2 Prepare the red and white border strips for blocks A and B (**A**):

- Short strips: Stitch 3-inch (7.6 cm) white strips on both sides of a background strip, and press the seams. Cut 100 strips that measure 1½ x 6½ inches (3.8 x 16.5 cm).

- Long strips: Stitch 4-inch (10.2 cm) white strips on both sides of a background strip, and press the seams. Cut 100 strips that measure 1½ x 8½ inches (3.8 x 16.5 cm).

making block A

3 For each block A, gather the following pieces:

- One 3½-inch (8.9 cm) center square cut from print fabric.

- Four matching 2⅜-inch (6 cm) squares cut from print fabric.

- One 4¼-inch (10.8 cm) square cut from background fabric.

- Four 2-inch (5.1 cm) squares cut from background fabric.

- Two short pieced strips.

- Two long pieced strips.

4 On the back of each small print square, draw a diagonal line from corner to opposite corner. Place two of these squares on top of the large background square, right sides together, as shown (**B**). Stitch ¼ inch (6 mm) on both sides of the drawn line, then cut on the line and press the fabrics open.

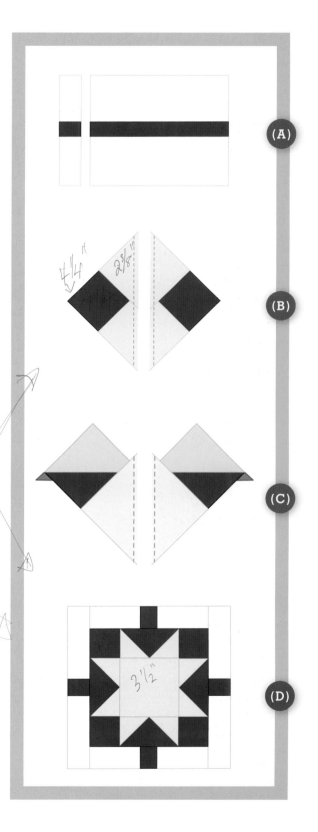

(A)

(B)

(C)

(D)

5 Place a small marked square on top of the remaining corner of each background square (which has now been cut in half to form a triangle), with right sides together **(C)**. Stitch ¼ inch (6 mm) on both sides of the drawn line, then cut on the line and press the fabrics open. You will now have four "flying geese" units.

6 Lay out the flying geese units, center square, and corner squares to form the block. Stitch the units together in each row, then join the rows. Square up the finished 6½-inch (16.5 cm) block as needed.

7 Stitch two short strips on opposite sides of the star block. Stitch two long strips on the remaining two sides **(D)**.

8 Repeat steps 3 through 7 to make a total of 40 block A pieces.

making block B

9 For each block B, gather the following pieces:

- One 6½-inch (16.5 cm) square cut from background fabric.
- One short pieced strip.
- One long pieced strip.
- Two 3 x 1½–inch (7.6 x 3.8 cm) white strips.

10 Lay out the pieces to form the block **(E)**. Stitch the strips above and below the center square, then attach the side strips. Press.

11 Repeat steps 9 through 11 to make a total of 20 block B pieces.

assembling the quilt top

12 Follow the assembly diagram (page 118) to stitch the blocks together, with a strip of sashing between each block and between rows. Press seams toward the red sashing.

13 Trim the corner blocks ¼ inch (6 mm) from the center of each block **(F)**. The finished quilt top should measure approximately 62 inches (157.5 cm) square.

14 Make a quilt sandwich with the quilt top, batting, and backing, and quilt as desired.

15 Stitch the binding strips together end-to-end to make one long strip and bind the quilt (pages 15–17).

dave's placemats

These patchwork placemats reinterpret the traditional Star of David motif in a contemporary way that's simple to piece, fresh to behold, and utterly functional.

handmade by MALKA DUBRAWSKY

fabric & such

- 1 fat quarter (45.7 x 55.9 cm) of cotton print fabric
- ½ yard (.5 m) of solid white cotton fabric
- ½ yard (.5 m) of coordinating cotton print or solid fabric (for backing)
- ½ yard (.5 m) of coordinating solid cotton fabric (for binding)
- 1 piece of cotton batting, 24 x 30 inches (61 x 76.2 cm)

tools

Basic Patchwork Kit (page 9)

Dinner plate

finished size

16½ x 24 inches (41.9 x 61 cm)

seam allowance

¼ inch (6 mm); press seam to one side, alternating sides where seams intersect.

get started

1 Cut out the following pieces from the fabrics:

From the cotton print fabric: 3 squares, each measuring 6½ inches (16.5 cm).

From the solid white cotton fabric:

- 3 squares, each measuring 6½ inches (16.5 cm)
- 12 squares, each measuring a generous 6⅛ inches (15.6 cm)

From the binding fabric:

- Strips cut on the bias, each measuring 1½ inches (3.8 cm).

2 Make six half-square triangles as follows:

- With right sides facing, pin two 6½-inch (16.5 cm) squares together, one white and one print.

- Use a pencil to mark a line from one corner of the square to the opposite diagonal corner.

- Stitch a seam ¼ inches (6 mm) from the pencil line, on both sides (A).

- Cut along the marked line. You now have two half-square triangles. Press seams to the print side.

- Repeat the process with the remaining 6¼-inch (12.7 cm) squares.

3 Working on a flat surface, lay out the half-square triangles and full squares, following the diagram (B). Working on the diagonal, start with the first row of three patches (squares) indicated. Stitch the patches together along the common edge and press the seams.

4 Continue in the same way, stitching the next two 5-patch rows, and the remaining 3-patch row.

5 Reassemble the rows in the correct order and stitch them together, each time matching up the side seams of the squares. Press.

6 Using a rotary cutter, ruler, and mat, trim the edges of the patchwork to a rectangle measuring 16½ x 24 inches (41.9 x 61 cm).

7 Make a quilt sandwich with the place mat top, batting, and backing, then pin or baste the layers together. Quilt the layers by hand or by machine, removing the basting as you work. The sample shows free-motion quilting, starting in the center and spiraling out to the edges.

8 Trim the layers flush. Use the dinner plate to draw rounded corners, then cut along the drawn lines.

9 Stitch the binding strips together end-to-end to make one long strip and bind the quilt (pages 15–17). Clip the seam allowance at the rounded corners before turning the binding to the back of the placemat.

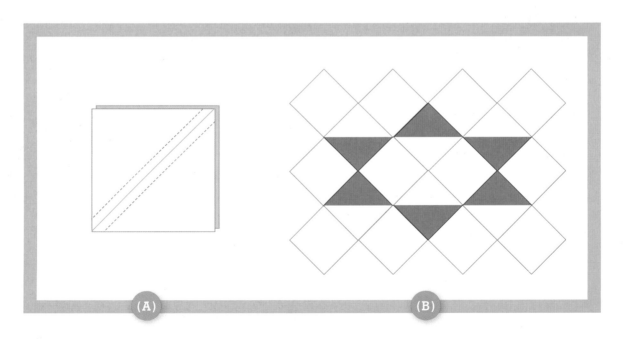

(A)   (B)

reindeer grove pillow

This patchwork pillowcase is as charming as it is cozy—the perfect hamlet for reindeer, gnomes, and all manner of magical holiday creatures.

handmade by **JOHN Q. ADAMS**

fabric & such

6 fat eighths of focus fabrics (for trees), each 9 x 22 inches (22.9 x 55.9 cm)

⅛ yard (.15 m) of brown fabric (for the tree trunks)

1 yard (.9 m) of linen (for background)

½ yard (.5 m) of red gingham fabric (for borders)

⅔ yard (.6 m) each of two fabrics (for backing panels)

⅔ yard (.6 m) of muslin, 54 inches (137.2 cm) wide

⅔ yard (.6 m) of batting

Binding tape (optional)

Pi low form, 20 x 50 inches (50.8 x 127 cm)

tools

Basic Patchwork Kit (page 9)

finished size

20 x 50 inches (50.8 x 127 cm)

seam allowance

¼ inch (6 mm) unless otherwise indicated

get started

1 Cut the following pieces from the fabrics.

From the focus fabrics: 16 rectangles, each measuring 5 x 6½ inches (12.7 x 16.5 cm). When cutting directional prints, the rectangles should be taller than they are wide.

From the brown fabric: 1 strip measuring 2½ inches (6.4 cm) x the width of the fabric.

From the linen background fabric:

- 3 strips, each measuring 10 inches (25.4 cm) x the width of the fabric. From those strips cut 16 rectangles, each measuring 6½ x 10 inches (16.5 x 25.4 cm).

- 2 strips, each measuring 2½ inches (6.4 cm) x the width of the fabric.

From the red border fabric:

- 2 strips, each measuring 2½ x 46½ inches (6.4 x 118.1 cm). You will likely have to join strips to achieve this length.

- 2 strips, each measuring 2½ x 20½ inches (6.4 x 52.1 cm).

From the backing panels:

- 1 piece measuring 20½ x 31½ inches (52.1 x 80 cm).

- 1 piece measuring 20½ x 41 inches (52.1 x 104.1 cm).

2 To make each tree block:

- Diagonally cut two of your background rectangles in half to create four triangles. Be careful to cut the two rectangles in opposite directions: the first from the top left to the bottom right, and the second from the bottom left to the top right (**A**). Set aside two of the triangles.

- Lay one of the cut triangles on top of a rectangle cut from a focus fabric, both with right sides up. Align the right angle of the background fabric with the right angle of the focus fabric's upper corner, with liberal overhang on the top, bottom, and left sides.

- It's not important for this alignment to be exact. This step employs a more liberal piecing technique. When using novelty fabric, be conscious of the print that will show in your final tree. The long edge of the triangle represents the sewn seam, giving you an idea of what part of the fabric will be showing in the final block.

- Carefully flip the triangle over on its long edge. Stitch ¼ inch (6 mm) from the triangle's long edge, joining the two pieces together (**B**).

- Use a ruler and rotary cutter to trim the excess fabric from the printed block along the triangle's long edge. Press the seam open.

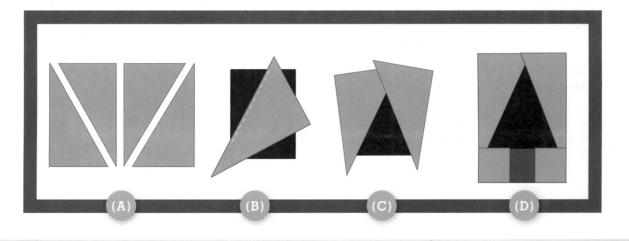

(A) (B) (C) (D)

- Repeat these steps on the opposite side of the block. Notice how this second triangle is at a slightly different angle than the first (C).

- Trim the block to 6½ inches square (16.5 cm). Use the bottom edge of the tree as a guide, or trim the block in any way you like to create variety from block to block. As long as the tree has a base, a point at the top more than a ¼ inch (6 mm) away from the top edge, and measures 6½ inches square (16.5 cm), it's a good block!

- Repeat to make 16 total tree blocks.

3 To create and add the tree trunks:

- P ece together the two 2½-inch (6.4 cm) linen strips with the 2½-inch (6.4 cm) brown fabric strip. Stitch the three strips together along their long edges, with the tree trunk fabric in between the two linen strips. Press seams open. The pieced strip will measure 6½ x 44 inches (16.5 x 111.8 cm).

- From this strip, cut 16 pieces that measure 6½ x 2¾ inches (16.5 x 7 cm).

- Stitch a tree trunk piece to the bottom of each 6½-inch (16.5 cm) tree block (D). Each completed block should measure 6½ x 8½ inches (16.5 x 21.6 cm).

- Repeat to sew trunks onto all 16 tree blocks.

4 Lay out the 16 tree blocks into two rows of eight trees each. Stitch the blocks into rows, then join the rows together, matching up the block seams.

5 Stitch the long border strips to the top and bottom edges of the blocks, trimming the strips to match the width of the pillow top. Press. Then stitch the remaining border strips to the left and right edges of the blocks. Press.

6 Make a quilt sandwich with the pillow top, batting, and muslin, and quilt as desired. The sample shows quilting with a horizontal stippling pattern to suggest a blowing wind.

7 To make the envelope-style back:

- Fold the 31½-inch (80 cm) backing panel in half lengthwise to make a rectangle measuring 20½ x 15¾ inches (52.1 x 40 cm). Press well to create a crisp folded end. If desired, bind the folded edge using the binding tape.

- Make a ¼-inch (6 mm) double-fold hem on one 20½-inch (52.1 cm) edge of the remaining backing panel. The hemmed backing panel will measure 20½ x 40½ inches (52.1 x 102.9 cm).

8 To assemble the pillow:

- Lay the smaller backing panel on top of the quilted pillow top, right sides together and aligning the raw 20½-inch (52.1 cm) edge of the backing panel with the left side of the pillow top.

- Lay the larger backing panel on top of both layers in the same way, aligning the backing panel with the right side of the pillow top. The backing panels will overlap approximately 7 inches (17.8 cm). Pin well around all four sides.

- Starting on one edge, stitch around all four sides of the pillow, pivoting at the corners and backstitching to lock the beginning and end of the stitches. You may want to stitch around twice for added strength. Snip the corners without cutting into your seam.

- Turn the pillow right side out and push out the corners.

- Inse t the pillow form, and you're done!

templates

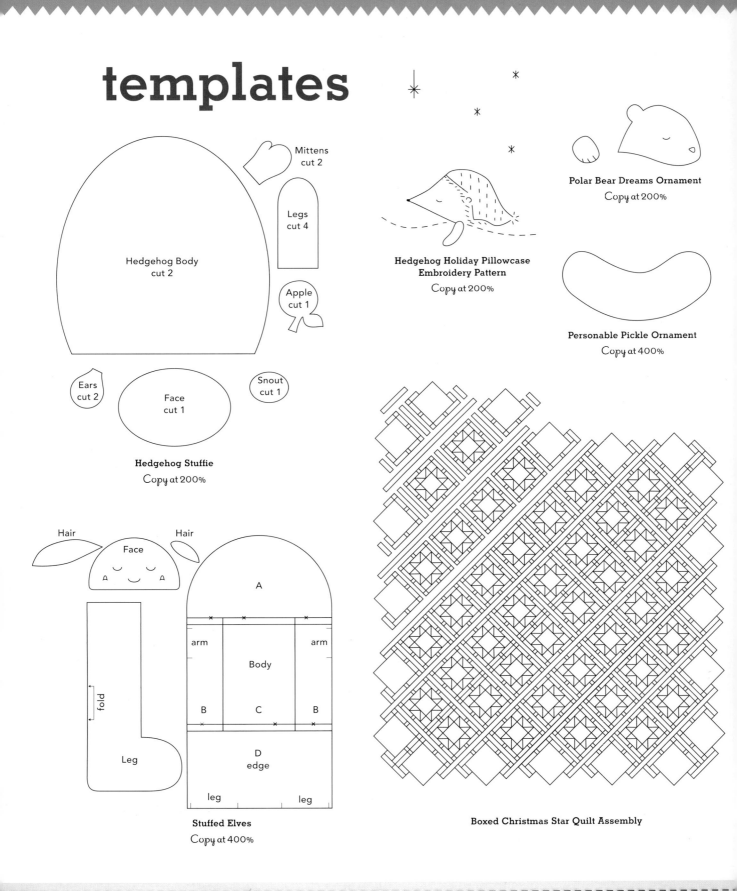

Mittens cut 2

Legs cut 4

Apple cut 1

Hedgehog Body cut 2

Ears cut 2

Face cut 1

Snout cut 1

Hedgehog Stuffie
Copy at 200%

Polar Bear Dreams Ornament
Copy at 200%

Hedgehog Holiday Pillowcase Embroidery Pattern
Copy at 200%

Personable Pickle Ornament
Copy at 400%

Hair   Face   Hair

fold

Leg

A

arm   arm

Body

B   C   B

D
edge

leg   leg

Stuffed Elves
Copy at 400%

Boxed Christmas Star Quilt Assembly

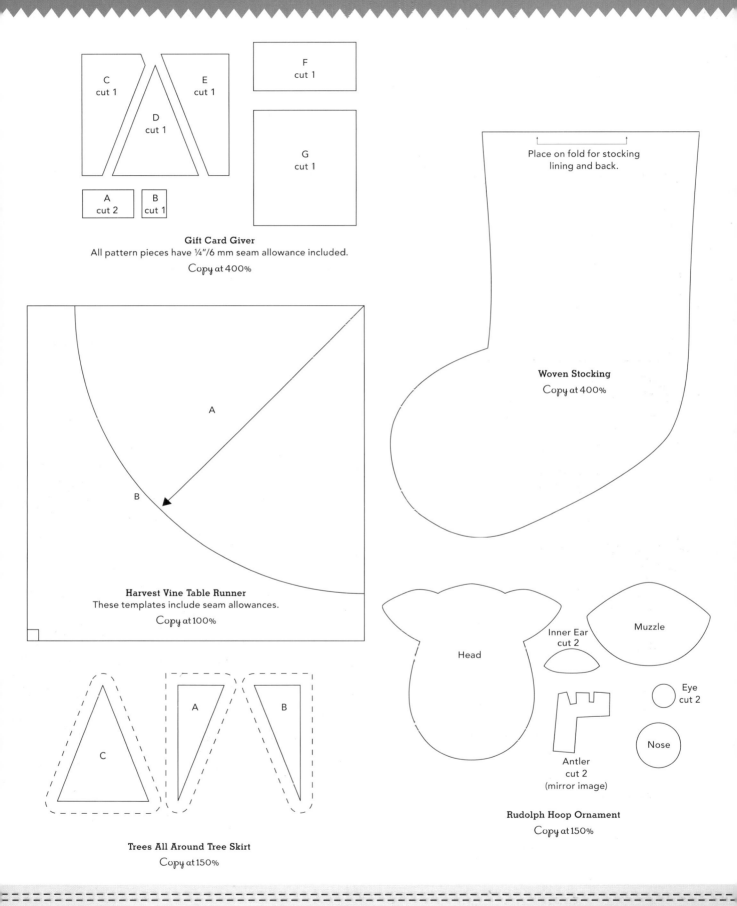

C
cut 1

E
cut 1

D
cut 1

F
cut 1

G
cut 1

A
cut 2

B
cut 1

Gift Card Giver
All pattern pieces have ¼"/6 mm seam allowance included.
Copy at 400%

A

B

Harvest Vine Table Runner
These templates include seam allowances.
Copy at 100%

Place on fold for stocking lining and back.

Woven Stocking
Copy at 400%

Head

Inner Ear
cut 2

Muzzle

Eye
cut 2

Nose

Antler
cut 2
(mirror image)

Rudolph Hoop Ornament
Copy at 150%

C

A

B

Trees All Around Tree Skirt
Copy at 150%

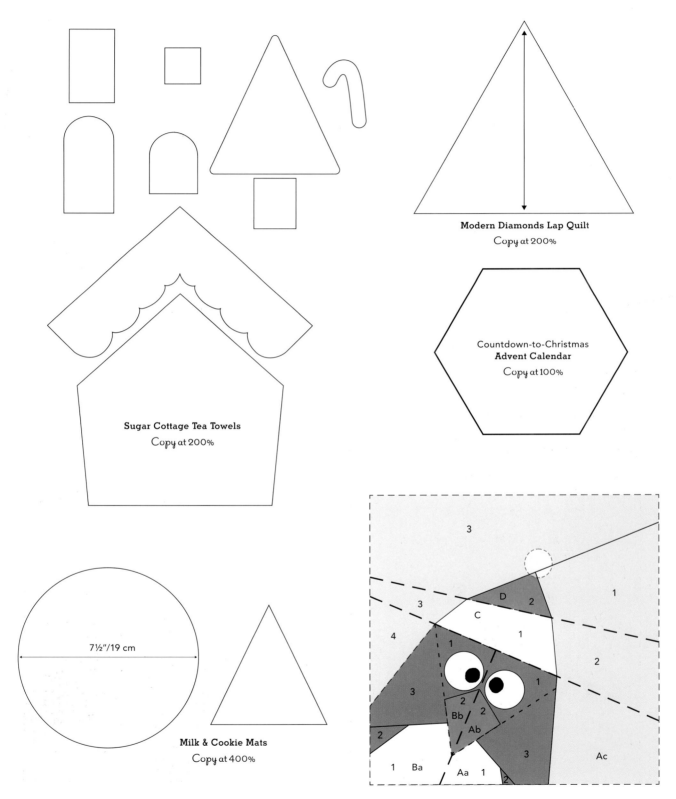

Modern Diamonds Lap Quilt
Copy at 200%

Countdown-to-Christmas
Advent Calendar
Copy at 100%

Sugar Cottage Tea Towels
Copy at 200%

7½"/19 cm

Milk & Cookie Mats
Copy at 400%

3

3
4

D
C
2
1
1

1
2

2

1
3
2
Bb
2
Ab
1

2
3
Ac

1 Ba
Aa 1
2

Greetings from Antarctica! Pillows
Copy at 400% for large; copy at 200% for small.

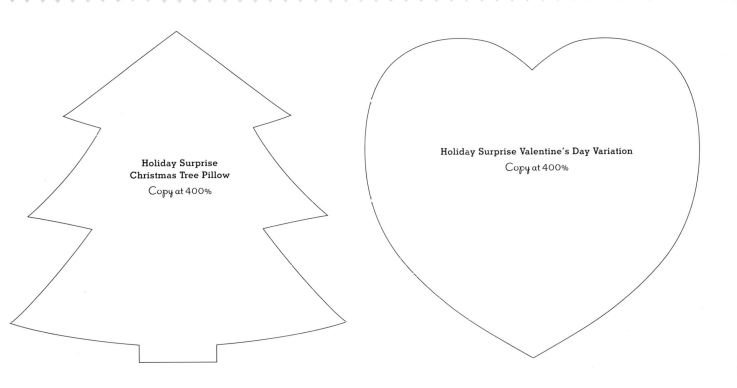

**Holiday Surprise
Christmas Tree Pillow**

Copy at 400%

Holiday Surprise Valentine's Day Variation

Copy at 400%

Bold dashed lines: Cut pattern apart into main lettered sections.
Light dashed lines: Cut pattern apart into lettered sub-sections.
Solid lines: Stitching lines.
Sew up each subsection, then piece them together in alphabetical order.

Add ¼-inch seam allowance to all sides of the cut fabric pieces.

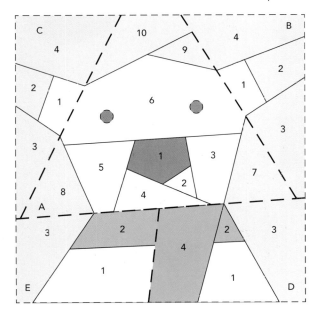

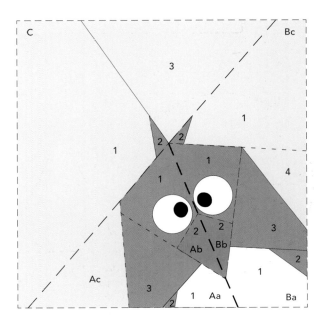

Greetings from Antarctica! Pillows
Copy at 400% for large; copy at 200% for small.

Home Squash Home Wall Hanging
Copy at 400%

Stem

Leaf

1 2 3 4 5

Home Squash
Embroidery Pattern

A

B

C

D
center circle

Modern Wreath Baby Quilt
Copy at 400%

ABCDEFGHI
JKLMNOPQR
STUVWXYZ
1234567890

Read Between the Lines Pillow Letter Templates
Graph paper squares = 1"/2.5 cm

Drawstring Wine Bag
Copy at 200%

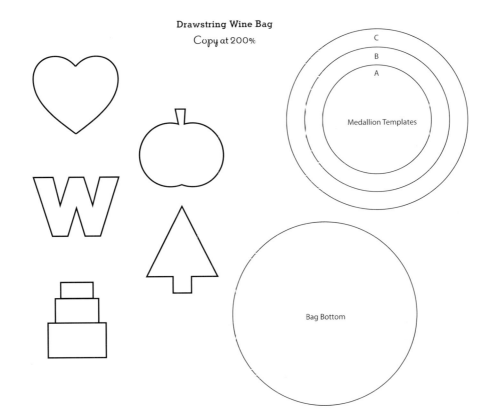

Medallion Templates

C
B
A

Bag Bottom

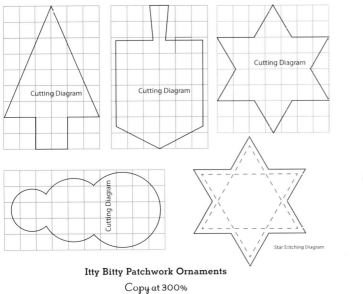

Cutting Diagram

Cutting Diagram

Cutting Diagram

Cutting Diagram

Star Stitching Diagram

Itty Bitty Patchwork Ornaments
Copy at 300%

run, run as fast as you can

Gingerbread Men Embroidered Apron
Copy at 300%

Fun Fun Holiday Bunting Chart

letter	red	white
A	(2) 7½inches (19 cm) (3) 3½ inches (8.9 cm) (2) 2½ inches (6.4 cm) (8) 1½ inches (3.8 cm) TOTAL: 42½ inches (108 cm)	(2) 4½ inches (11.4 cm) (6) 1½ inches (3.8 cm) TOTAL: 18 inches (45.7 cm)
B	(2) 7½ inches (19 cm) (2) 2½ inches (6.4 cm) (15) 1½ inches (3.8 cm) TOTAL: 42½ inches (108 cm)	(1) 5½ inches (14 cm) (4) 1½ inches (3.8 cm) TOTAL: 11½ inches (29.2 cm)
C	(2) 7½ inches (19 cm) (4) 3½ inches (8.89 cm) (10) 1½ inches (3.8 cm) TOTAL: 44 inches (111.8 cm)	(1) 5½ inches (14 cm) (11) 1½ inches (3.8 cm) TOTAL: 17½ inches (44.5 cm)
D	(2) 7½ inches (19 cm) (3) 3½ inches (8.9 cm) (2) 2½ inches (6.4 cm) (8) 1½ inches (3.8 cm) TOTAL: 42½ inches (108 cm)	(1) 5½ inches (14 cm) (1) 3½ inches (8.9 cm) (6) 1½ inches (3.8 cm) TOTAL: 18 inches (45.7 cm)
E	(2) 7½ inches (19 cm) (2) 3½ inches (8.9 cm) (14) 1½ inches (3.8 cm) TOTAL: 33 inches (83.8 cm)	(1) 5½ inches (14 cm) (10) 1½ inches (3.8 cm) TOTAL: 20½ inches (52.1 cm)
F	(2) 7½ inches (19 cm) (2) 5½ inches (14 cm) (2) 3½ inches (8.9 cm) (6) 1½ inches (3.8 cm) TOTAL: 42 inches (106.7 cm)	(1) 5½ inches (14 cm) (6) 1½ inches (3.8 cm) TOTAL: 14½ inches (36.8 cm)
G	(2) 7½ inches (19 cm) (2) 3½ inches (8.9 cm) (13) 1½ inches (3.8 cm) TOTAL: 28½ inches (72.4 cm)	(1) 5½ inches (14 cm) (1) 3½ inches (8.9 cm) (8) 1½ inches (3.8 cm) TOTAL: 21 inches (53.3 cm)
H	(2) 7½ inches (19 cm) (6) 3½ inches (8.9 cm) (4) 1½ inches (3.8 cm) TOTAL: 42 inches (106.7 cm)	(2) 5½ inches (14 cm) (3) 1½ inches (3.8 cm) TOTAL: 15½ inches (39.4 cm)
I	(2) 7½ inches (19 cm) (4) 3½ inches (8.9 cm) (10) 1½ inches (3.8 cm) TOTAL: 44 inches (111.8 cm)	(1) 5½ inches (14 cm) (8) 1½ inches (3.8 cm) TOTAL: 17½ inches (44.5 cm)
J	(2) 7½ inches (19 cm) (3) 5½ inches (14 cm) (1) 4½ inches (11.4 cm) (6) 1½ inches (3.8 cm) TOTAL: 37 inches (94 cm)	(1) 5½ inches (14 cm) (6) 1½ inches (3.8 cm) TOTAL: 14½ inches (36.8 cm)
K	(2) 7½ inches (19 cm) (5) 3½ inches (8.9 cm) (2) 2½ inches (6.4 cm) (5) 1½ inches (3.8 cm) TOTAL: 45 inches (114.3 cm)	(1) 5½ inches (14 cm) (9) 1½ inches (3.8 cm) TOTAL: 19 inches (48.3 cm)
L	(2) 7½ inches (19 cm) (4) 5½ inches (14 cm) (6) 1½ inches (3.8 cm) TOTAL: 46 inches (116.8 cm)	(1) 5½ inches (14 cm) (4) 1½ inches (3.8 cm) TOTAL: 11½ inches (29.2 cm)
M	(2) 7½ inches (19 cm) (2) 4½ inches (11.4 cm) (2) 3½ inches (8.9 cm) (2) 2½ inches (6.4 cm) (4) 1½ inches (3.8 cm) TOTAL: 42 inches (106.7 cm)	(2) 5½ inches (14 cm) (3) 1½ inches (3.8 cm) TOTAL: 15½ inches (39.4 cm)
N	(2) 7½ inches (19 cm) (2) 4½ inches (11.4 cm) (2) 3½ inches (8.9 cm) (2) 2½ inches (6.4 cm) (4) 1½ inches (3.8 cm) TOTAL: 42 inches (106.7 cm)	(2) 5½ inches (14 cm) (3) 1½ inches (3.8 cm) TOTAL: 15½ inches (39.4 cm)
O	(2) 7½ inches (19 cm) (3) 3½ inches (8.9 cm) (10) 1½ inches (3.8 cm) TOTAL: 40½ inches (102.9)	(2) 5½inches (14 cm) (6) 1½ inches (3.8 cm) TOTAL: 20 inches (50.8 cm)
P	(2) 7½ inches (19 cm) (4) 3½ inches (8.9 cm) (9) 1½ inches (3.8 cm) TOTAL: 42½ inches (108 cm)	(1) 5½ inches (14 cm) (1) 3½ inches (8.9 cm) (6) 1½ inches (3.8 cm) TOTAL: 18 inches (45.7 cm)
Q	(2) 7½ inches (19 cm) (1) 5½ inches (14 cm) (6) 2½ inches (6.4 cm) (5) 1½ inches (3.8 cm) TOTAL: 43 inches (109.2 cm)	(2) 4½ inches (11.4 cm) (5) 1½ inches (3.8 cm) TOTAL: 16½ inches (41.9 cm)
R	(2) 7½ inches (19 cm) (2) 3½ inches (8.9 cm) (1) 2½ inches (6.4 cm) (11) 1½ inches (3.8 cm) TOTAL: 41 inches (104.1 cm)	(1) 5½ inches (14 cm) (1) 3½ inches (8.9 cm) (1) 2½ inches (6.4 cm) (7) 1½ inches (3.8 cm) TOTAL: 22 inches (55.9 cm)
S	(2) 7½ inches (19 cm) (18) 1½ inches (3.8 cm) TOTAL: 42 inches (106.7 cm)	(2) 3½ inches (8.9 cm) (11) 1½ inches (3.8 cm) TOTAL: 23½ inches (59.7 cm)
T	(2) 7½ inches (19 cm) (4) 5½ inches (14 cm) (6) 1½ inches (3.8 cm) TOTAL: 46 inches (116.8 cm)	(1) 5½ inches (14 cm) (4) 1½ inches (3.8 cm) TOTAL: 1½ inches (29.2 cm)
U	(2) 7½ inches (19 cm) (3) 5½ inches (14 cm) (7) 1½ inches (3.8 cm) TOTAL: 27 inches (68.6 cm)	(2) 5½ inches (14 cm) (3) 1½ inches (3.8 cm) TOTAL: 15½ inches (39.4 cm)
V	(2) 7½ inches (19 cm) (1) 5½ inches (14 cm) (2) 4½ inches (11.4 cm) (2) 3½ inches (8.9 cm) (2) 2½ inches (6.4 cm) (3) 1½ inches (3.8 cm) TOTAL: 46 inches (116.8 cm)	(2) 3½ inches (8.9 cm) (3) 1½ inches (3.8 cm) TOTAL: 11½ inches (29.2 cm)
W	(2) 7½ inches (19 cm) (2) 4½ inches (11.4 cm) (2) 3½ inches (8.9 cm) (2) 2½ inches (6.4 cm) (4) 1½ inches (3.8 cm) TOTAL: 42 inches (106.7 cm)	(2) 5½ inches (14 cm) (3) 1½ inches (3.8 cm) TOTAL: 15½ inches (39.4 cm)
X	(2) 7½ inches (19 cm) (4) 3½ inches (8.9 cm) (4) 2½ inches (6.4 cm) (6) 1½ inches (3.8 cm) TOTAL: 48 inches (121.9 cm)	(9) 1½ inches (3.8 cm) TOTAL: 13½ inches (34.3 cm)
Y	(2) 7½ inches (19 cm) (3) 4½ inches (11.4 cm) (4) 3½ inches (8.9 cm) (3) 1½ inches (3.8 cm) TOTAL: 47 inches (119.4 cm)	(3) 2½ inches (6.4 cm) (2) 1½ inches (3.8 cm) TOTAL: 10½ inches (26.7 cm)
Z	(2) 7½ inches (19 cm) (2) 4½ inches (11.4 cm) (2) 3½ inches (8.9 cm) (2) 2½ inches (6.4 cm) (4) 1½ inches (3.8 cm) TOTAL: 42 inches (106.7 cm)	(2) 5½ inches (14 cm) (3) 1½ inches (3.8 cm) TOTAL: 15½ inches (39.4 cm)

about the author

John Q. Adams is a husband and father of three who enjoys sewing and quilting in his spare time. Inspired by the growing number of crafting blogs and the emergence of vibrant, modern quilting fabrics in the textile industry, John convinced his wife to teach him how to use her sewing machine in 2004 and hasn't looked back. He started his popular blog, QuiltDad.com, in 2008 to share his love of patchwork with others.

Since then, John has become very active in the online quilting communities. Today, he applies his modern quilting aesthetic by designing quilt patterns for both fabric designers and companies and contributing frequently to creative blogs, books, and other collaborative endeavors. John is also a co-founder of the popular e-magazine Fat Quarterly.

John was born and raised in Brooklyn, New York, and currently lives in Holly Springs, North Carolina, with his wife, Kiely, twin daughters, Megan and Bevin, and son, Sean. He earned his undergraduate and master's degrees at the University of North Carolina at Chapel Hill and, when he isn't sewing, enjoys cheering for the UNC Tar Heels.

acknowledgments

I would like to first thank the many talented craft makers, bloggers, and designers who give freely of their time, talent, and creative spirit on a daily basis, many of whom are included in this book. You have educated, inspired, and influenced me through the years. Though there are too many to name, I'd like to extend special thanks to Amanda Jean and Jacquie, whose blogs are among the first and (still) the best that I've read. Without your support, encouragement, and generosity, I may never have taken those first critical steps on the creative journey that has led me here.

Thanks also to Katy, Tacha, and Brioni—my awesome Fat Quarterly teammates— for having a bold vision, the discipline to see it through, the talent to make it beautiful, and the confidence to bring me along for the ride.

Special thanks to Amanda Carestio and the amazing team at Lark Crafts for your expertise, guidance, and endless patience in bringing this book to life. You're the best at what you do, as evidenced by the beauty in the end result. Thank you!

I would like to thank my family, especially my mother, father, and brother, for always believing in and promoting the importance of creativity and the arts, and for encouraging me to listen to my own creative voice.

Thanks to my three beautiful children, who inspire me every day—not only in my craft, but in my desire to be the best man that I can be.

To my beautiful wife, who is my biggest fan and reminds me on a daily basis that anything is possible if you choose to chase your dreams: thanks for supporting me every day as I chase mine. I love you!

And finally, thanks to all of you, not only for reading this, but for being active members of the creative and handmade community. Keep sewing, keep quilting, and keep following your dreams.

about the designers

Dorreen Agres is a Cytotechnologist working full-time at a private pathology laboratory specializing in cancer screening. She began quilting in 2002 as a way of de-stressing from her day job. Little did Dorreen realize the first day she entered a quilt shop, there is no going back. Not only did she fall in love with the quilting process, she found a wonderful community of like-minded crafters and made friends along the way. Dorreen is a former sample quilter from the local quilt shop and is currently a volunteer quilter for the local Quilts of Valor.

Nicole Vos van Avezathe (of Follow the White Bunny) lives with her family in the Netherlands. She makes original hand embroidery and craft patterns in her own style: sometimes odd, often sweet, and always unique. When not sewing, Nicole loves to write about her crafting adventures online. Learn more about Nicole and her patterns at her website, www.Followthewhitebunny.com.

Jeni Baker has been an avid sewer for the last ten years, and she loves nothing more than to be surrounded by fabric. A Marketing and Studio Art student living in Northeast Ohio with her bunny, George, Jeni's favorite part of the sewing process is fabric and color selection. In addition to sewing, Jeni's hobbies include photography, quilting, and collecting vintage kitchenware and bed sheets. Jeni blogs online at http://incolororder.blogspot.com and her projects and photographs of her works can be found at http://ironsea.etsy.com and http://flickr.com/photos/jenib.

Mo Bedell learned to sew from her Grandma Lydia who was an inspired and amazing seamstress; her Granny Mop was an art rep and collector. One shared with her a love of creating while the other showed her an appreciation for beautiful work, influences which have worked in tandem to inspire a lifelong love of creating and a freedom to really enjoy the work she does. Mo designs fabric for Timeless Treasures and loves designing sewing patterns for various publications. She blogs about the things she makes and does at www.limegardenias.blogspot.com.

Marilyn Butler is a wife, mother of four, and grandmother of two (soon to be four) who loves anything and everything creative. Throughout the years, Marilyn's creative aspirations have led her to create a variety of projects, including home decorations, clothing, and toys for her children and grandchildren. Marilyn's most recent passion is quilting because it gives her the delight of playing with color and design. In addition to quilting, Marilyn enjoys embroidery, collage, and other paper arts. When she's not busy crafting, she enjoys traveling with her husband. Marilyn is a member of the Kansas City Modern Quilt guild and participates in a variety of online quilting groups. Learn more about Marilyn's work by visiting her blog, http://marilynbutler.blogspot.com.

Sonja Callaghan has been sewing, knitting, and crocheting since childhood. She has always had a chronic obsession with mastering new creative skills and crafting quirky, fun, and beautiful handmade pieces. Sonja's current projects focus on pattern designing and she finds inspiration in strong graphic photographs, beautifully composed portraits, and vintage art. A sudden discovery of a striking natural palette has been known to stop her in her tracks and produce the tattered sketchbook from her purse. Sonja's pieces have turned up in a variety of exotic locales, from sofas throughout North America, to walls in the Australian outback and quilt guild meetings in Portugal. Some of her designs can also be found in recent publications by Stash books and Quiltmaker Magazine. Check out Sonja's website, http://artisania.wordpress.com, to see more of her work, including traveling gnomes, quirky farm critters, and a cast of funky Halloween characters.

Amanda Carestio's latest crafting obsessions include mini quilts and furniture makeovers. When she's not bent over her sewing machine or exploring the Blue Ridge Mountains, Amanda enjoys spending quality time with her husband and super-spoiled canines in Asheville, North Carolina. As a member of Lark's Needlearts team, Amanda's designs appear in several Lark books, and she is the author of *Fa La La La Felt*, *Stash Happy: Felt*, and

Heart-Felt Holidays. In addition to these publications, Amanda blogs online at http://www.LarkCrafts.com and at www.digsandbean.blogspot.com.

Jennifer Davis is a stay-at-home mom, military wife, and graduate student. She was raised in a one-stoplight Idaho farm town and now lives outside of Washington, D.C. She spent her teen years dying to get out of a small town, and now she's dying to get back in. She loves quilting, cooking, reading, and loving her babies. She harbors a secret dream of being a square dancer and sewing her own dancing outfits (*shhh*). She blogs at www.SugarStitches.com/blog.

Malka Dubrawsky first discovered the world of crafting in an eighth-grade art class. She moved on to graduate from college with a Bachelor's in Fine Arts in Studio Art. Her interest in textiles sprang from spending time at home with her children. Malka spent several years working primarily as a fiber artist, but more recently, Malka has been designing more functional textiles, though she continues to primarily use her own hand-dyed and patterned fabrics. To this end, Malka has directed her attentions towards designing quilts, pillows, and other various sundries that can be found at her online store http://stitchindye.etsy.com. Malka writes and designs patterns and has been published in multiple magazines and several books. Her first book, *Color Your Cloth: A Quilter's Guide to Dyeing and Patterning Fabric*, was published by Lark Books in November of 2009 and a second book, *Fresh Quilting: Fearless, Color, Design, and Inspiration* was released in December 2010 by Interweave Press. Read more about Malka and her work at http://stitchindye.blogspot.com.

Cathy Gaubert is a wife, momma, maker of things, and the author of *Pretty in Patchwork: Doll Quilts* from Lark Crafts. Her days are filled with the antics of three sweet girlies, and her kitchen table is filled with more works in progress than you can shake a stick at. Peer into her world at www.handmadecathygaubert.blogspot.com, and do be sure to say hello.

Scott Hansen of Blue Nickel Studios (www.bluenickel-studios.com) has been creating stuff all his life, mostly messes, but now and then something good turns up. A self-taught quilter, Scott designs quilt patterns for magazines, fabric companies, and retail. His first book is due out sometime in 2012. Scott's inspiration comes from his quiet country mouse/city mouse life in the Pacific Northwest, United States. Luckily the rain there keeps him indoors often enough to get some sewing done...and "research" online for his blog and the new blogazine Generation Q. The Blue Nickel Studios tag line is "Urban Folk –Modern Design, Timeless Style," and Scott is known for his bold use of color and design.

Terri Harlan is a former mortgage lender turned mommy. Now with 18 years of sewing under her belt, Terri finds joy in helping others get inspired by blogging at www.Sew-Fantastic.blogspot.com. She's also a founding member of her local Modern Quilt Guild in Bakersfield, CA.

Jessica Kovach is a stay-at-home mother of three living near Lake Michigan in western Michigan. She learned to sew at an early age simply by watching her mother work and throughout the years has taught others her craft. One of Jessica's favorite aspects of quilting is the ability to design new patterns and experiment with a variety of colors for each new project. Jessica employs her skills to make children's clothing and home décor items, and to design new appliqué and quilting patterns. When she's not quilting, Jessica enjoys spending time with her husband and children. To see more of Jessica's work, visit her blog Twin Fibers at www.twinfibers.blogspot.com.

Christina Lane is a longarm quilter and pattern designer living in Ridgefield, WA. In addition to quilting, Christina enjoys photography, knitting, and doodling. When not quilting, she enjoys spending her days at home with her son. Follow Christina on her blog, The Sometimes Crafter, as www.thesometimescrafter.com.

Kelly Lautenbach is a loving wife and empty nester that spends her days pretending to run her husband's business and regularly sneaking over to her studio. Time flies by as she creates all sorts of fabric-y goodness. As dinnertime nears, Kelly slips back into the "real world" just in time to make it look as if she spent the day working. Her former life as a scrap-booker has served Kelly well in her foray into the world of fabric and quilting. Her creative background continues to influence many of her current projects. When not sewing, Kelly enjoys living the good life in Nebraska and playing Gram to the world's cutest little boy, Sutton.

Angela Mitchell is a former elementary school teacher living in snowy northwest Pennsylvania with her husband and three children. A self-taught crafter, Angela has been sewing for over twelve years. Her favorite things to design and create are pillows and quilts. When she's not crafting, Angela enjoys spending the day at home with her children. Visit Angela online at http://fussycut.blogspot.com to see more of her work and read about her creative processes.

Kaye Prince, librarian by day, moonlights as a designer in her spare time. She spends most of her time outside the library quilting up a storm and designing new patterns. Follow Kaye on her online blog, miss-print.blogspot.com.

Charlie Scott and Ryan Walsh are self-taught quilters and quilt designers who enjoy mixing traditional block patterns with modern design aesthetics. Together, they are the driving force behind Patchwork Squared and strive to bring fresh, new ideas that inspire and get people excited about quilting. To learn more about the guys and their thoughts on quilting, visit www.patchworksquared.com.

Monica Solorio-Snow spends much of her free time avoiding cooking, gardening and home keeping—and fills every spare minute nestled inside her Happy Zombie Hideaway (sewing room) at her home in Astoria, Oregon. Continually concocting ways to spend more time quilting, home-sewing and crafting, Top Ramen and Cheerio's are a dinner staple in the Solorio-Snow home. Monica is a freelance quilt and home-sewing pattern designer, as well as fabric designer for Lecien Fabrics of Japan. Monica can be found blogging and tweeting via thehappyzombie.com.

Amanda Woodward-Jennings is the founder of msmcporkchopquilts.com and the co-owner of The Frosted Pumpkin Stitchery. Amanda loves quilting and is obsessed with candy. When she's not quilting or sewing up a storm, Amanda spends time in the kitchen, baking and canning for her husband, Porkchop.

Index

Also in this series:

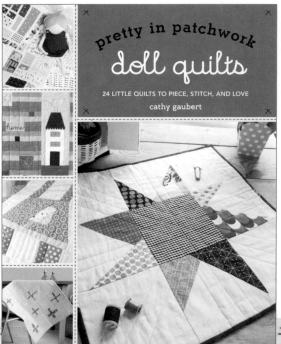